Exploring the Basic Income Guarantee

Series Editor
Karl Widerquist
Georgetown University in Qatar
Doha, Qatar

Basic income is one of the most innovative, powerful, straightforward, and controversial proposals for addressing poverty and growing inequalities. A Basic Income Guarantee (BIG) is designed to be an unconditional, government-insured guarantee that all citizens will have enough income to meet their basic needs. The concept of basic, or guaranteed, income is a form of social provision and this series examines the arguments for and against it from an interdisciplinary perspective with special focus on the economic and social factors. By systematically connecting abstract philosophical debates over competing principles of BIG to the empirical analysis of concrete policy proposals, this series contributes to the fields of economics, politics, social policy, and philosophy and establishes a theoretical framework for interdisciplinary research. It will bring together international and national scholars and activists to provide a comparative look at the main efforts to date to pass unconditional BIG legislation across regions of the globe and will identify commonalities and differences across countries drawing lessons for advancing social policies in general and BIG policies in particular.

More information about this series at
http://www.palgrave.com/gp/series/14981

Karl Widerquist

A Critical Analysis of Basic Income Experiments for Researchers, Policymakers, and Citizens

palgrave
macmillan

Karl Widerquist
Georgetown University in Qatar
Doha, Qatar

Exploring the Basic Income Guarantee
ISBN 978-3-030-03848-9 ISBN 978-3-030-03849-6 (eBook)
https://doi.org/10.1007/978-3-030-03849-6

Library of Congress Control Number: 2018963169

This Palgrave Pivot imprint is published by the registered company Springer Nature Switzerland AG
The registered company address is: Gewerbestrasse 11, 6330 Cham, Switzerland

Acknowledgments

I would like to give special thanks to Zohaib Tahir, my research assistant, who provided incredibly useful help. I would also like to thank Misba Bhatti, Zahra Barbar, Mehran Kamrava, and everyone at Center for International and Regional Studies (CIRS) for funding and organizing a workshop on this book, for funding my research assistant, for showing so much confidence in me, and for giving me a deadline to finish the first draft quickly. Thanks to the 11 people who came to the CIRS workshop and gave feedback that made me rewrite this book: Justin Gengler, Soumya Kapoor, John Gal, Simon Wigley, Jamie Cooke, Sarath Davala, Olli Kangasa, Loek Groot, Nisreen Salti, Mimi Ajzenstadt, and Robert van der Veen. Thanks also to Kate McFarland, Ron Hikel, and Karsten Lieberkind for especially useful comments. Thanks to everyone who attended my various presentations of these ideas and gave me feedback, especially in the two small-group presentations I made at Georgetown University in Qatar.

Contents

About the Author

Karl Widerquist holds doctorates in Political Theory and Economics, but is Associate Professor of Philosophy at Georgetown University in Qatar. He specializes in distributive justice—the ethics of who has what. *The Atlantic Monthly* called him "a leader of the worldwide basic income movement." Dozens of articles and seven books authored by him have been published, including *Independence, Propertylessness, and Basic Income: A Theory of Freedom as the Power to Say No*. He cofounded US Basic Income Guarantee (USBIG) (the first basic income network in the United States) in 1999, *Basic Income Studies* (the first academic journal dedicated to basic income) in 2006, and *Basic Income News* (the first news website dedicated to basic income) in 2012. He served as co-chair of the Basic Income Earth Network from 2010 to 2017. He writes the blog *The Indepentarian* for *Basic Income News*. His previous writings on basic income experiments include "A Failure to Communicate: What (If Anything) Can We Learn from the Negative Income Tax Experiments?" (*The Journal of Socio-Economics* [2005]) and "The Bottom Line in a Basic Income Experiment" (*Basic Income Studies* [2006]). You can reach him at karl@widerquist.com.

List of Tables

CHAPTER 1

Introduction

Abstract This chapter introduces and previews the book with a broad overview of the problems involved in conducting Universal Basic Income (UBI) experiments and in reporting the results in ways that successfully increase public understanding of the issue. It argues that experimenters should work backward from the big "bottom-line questions" that are most important to the public discussion of UBI to the variables that tests can actually address, and then forward again, closely explaining the relationship between experimental findings and the things people discussing UBI as a potential national policy really want to know.

Keywords Basic income experiments • Negative Income Tax experiments • Social science experiments • Basic income • Universal Basic Income • Inequality • Poverty

"The devil's in the details" is a common saying about policy *proposals*. Perhaps we need a similar saying about policy *research*—for example, "the devil's in the caveats." No simple list of caveats can bridge the enormous gap in understanding between the specialists who conduct policy research and the citizens and policymakers who are responsible for policy but often have overblown expectations about what policy research can do.

K. Widerquist, *A Critical Analysis of Basic Income Experiments for Researchers, Policymakers, and Citizens*, Exploring the Basic Income Guarantee, https://doi.org/10.1007/978-3-030-03849-6_1

Consider this headline from *MIT Technology Review*, December 2016, "In 2017, We Will Find Out If a Basic Income Makes Sense."[1] At the time, several countries were preparing to conduct experiments on the Universal Basic Income (UBI)—a policy to put a floor under everyone's income. But none of the experiments had plans to release any findings at all in 2017 (nor did they). The more important inaccuracy of this article was that it reflected the common but naïve belief that UBI experiments are capable of determining whether UBI "makes sense." Social science experiments can produce useful information, but they cannot answer the big questions that most interest policymakers and voters, such as does UBI work or should we introduce it.

The limited contribution that social science experiments can make to big policy questions like these would not be a problem if everyone understood it, but unfortunately, the article in *MIT Technology Review* is no anomaly. It's a good example of the misreporting on UBI and related experiments that has gone on for decades.[2] *MIT Technology Review* was founded at the Massachusetts Institute of Technology in 1899. Its website promises "intelligent, lucid, and authoritative … journalism … by a knowledgeable editorial staff, governed by a policy of accuracy and independence."[3] Although *the Review*'s expertise is in technology rather than in scientific research, it is the kind of publication nonspecialists expect can help them understand the limits and usefulness of scientific research.

Policy discussion, policy research, and policymaking involve diverse groups of people with widely differing backgrounds: citizens, journalists, academics, elected officials, and appointed public servants (call these last two "policymakers"). Although some people fit more than one group, the groups as a whole don't have enough shared background knowledge to achieve mutual understanding of what research implies about policy. Researchers often do not understand what citizens and policymakers expect from research, while citizens and policymakers often do not understand the inherent difficulties of policy research or the difference between what research shows and what they want to know.

[1] Jamie Condliffe, "In 2017, We Will Find out If a Basic Income Makes Sense," *MIT Technology Review*, December 19, 2016.

[2] Karl Widerquist, "A Failure to Communicate: What (If Anything) Can We Learn from the Negative Income Tax Experiments?," *The Journal of Socio-Economics* 34, no. 1 (2005).

[3] *MIT Technology Review*, "What We Do," *MIT Technology Review*.

Specialists usually include a list of caveats covering the limitations of their research, but caveats are incapable of doing the work researchers often rely on them to do. A dense, dull, and lengthy list of caveats cannot provide nonspecialists with a firm grasp of what research does and does not imply about the policy at issue. Therefore, even the best scientific policy research can leave nonspecialists with an oversimplified, or simply wrong, impression of its implications for policy. People who do not understand the limits of experiments also cannot understand the value that experiments do have.

Better-written, longer, or clearer caveats won't solve the problem either. The communication problem, coupled with the inherent limitations of social science experimentation, calls for a different approach to bridge the gap in understanding.

This book considers how these sorts of problems might affect future UBI experiments and suggests ways way to avoid them. As later chapters explain, UBI has many complex economic, political, social, and cultural effects that cannot be observed in any small-scale, controlled experiment. Even the best UBI experiment makes only a small contribution to the body of knowledge on the issue. It addresses questions only partially and indirectly while leaving many others unanswered.

Citizens and policymakers considering introducing UBI are understandably interested in larger issues. They want answers to the big questions, such as does UBI work as intended; is it cost-effective; should we introduce it on a national level? The gap between what an experiment can show and the answers to these big questions is enormous. Within one field, specialists can often achieve mutual understanding of this gap with no more than a simple list of caveats, many of which are self-evident and need not be mentioned. Across different fields, mutual understanding quickly gets more difficult, and it becomes extremely difficult between groups as diverse as the people involved in the discussion of UBI and those involved in the discussion of UBI experiments.

The process that brought about the experiments in most countries is not likely to produce research focused on bridging that gap in understanding. The demand for the current round of experiments seems to be driven more by the desire to have a UBI experiment than by the desire to learn anything specific about UBI from an experiment. An unfocused demand for a test puts researchers in position to learn whatever an experiment can show, whether or not it is closely connected to what citizens and policymakers most want to know.

The vast majority of research specialists who conduct experiments are not fools or fakers. They will look for evidence that makes a positive and useful contribution to the body of knowledge about UBI. But the effort to translate that contribution into a better public understanding of the body of evidence about UBI is far more difficult than often recognized. This communication problem badly affected many past experiments and is in danger of happening again.

To understand the difficulty of the task, imagine a puzzle strewn out over the floor of a large, dark, locked room. A map of the entire puzzle, assembled together, provides answers to the big questions—does it work, and should we implement it? An experiment shines a light through a window, lighting up some of the puzzle pieces, so that researchers can attempt to map how they might fit together. They can easily map the pieces near the window, but further away, their view gets dimmer, the accuracy of their map decreases, and in dark corners of the room many pieces remain unobservable.

Although scientists like to solve entire puzzles when possible, under normal circumstances, they have to settle for something less ambitious. That's why the basic goal of scientific research is to increase the sum of knowledge available to the scientific community—even if that increase is very small. In terms of the example, a research project can achieve the basic goal by mapping even one new piece, even if the puzzle as a whole remains unsolved and the map is only readable to other scientists.

As the *MIT Review* article illustrates, nonspecialists tend to expect something far more definitive, as if a social science experiment had the same goal as a high school science test: to determine whether the subject passes or fails. People often expect research to produce an estimate of whether UBI works or whether the country should introduce it. In terms of the metaphor, they expect researchers to provide their best estimate of the solution to the entire puzzle.

If researchers present their findings in the normal way for social scientists, they present something fundamentally different from what citizens and policymakers are looking for and possibly expecting. The potential for misunderstanding is enormous when research reports say something to the effect of *here are the parts of the puzzle we were able to map* to an audience looking for something to the effect of *here is our best estimate of the solution to the entire puzzle*. Caveats do not and cannot draw the necessary connection, which requires something more to the effect of *here is how the parts we were able to map can be used toward a larger effort to find the solution to the entire puzzle and how close or far we remain from it.*

In research reports, caveats typically focus not on the connection between the two goals, but on trying to help people understand research on its own terms. In the analogy, caveats tend to focus on the areas that experiments were able to map: how did they map this area; what does it mean to map this area; how accurate is the map of this area, and so on. The relationship between the areas mapped and the solution to the whole puzzle is often covered by one big caveat so seemingly simple that it often goes unstated: the areas we mapped are far from a solution to the entire puzzle. In other words, the information gathered about UBI in an experiment is far from a definitive, overall evaluation of UBI as a policy. As obvious as that caveat might be to researchers, it is not at all obvious to many nonspecialists.

Of course, nonspecialists know there are some caveats about the reliability of the experiment, but if they overlook or misunderstand that one big caveat, they will nevertheless believe that researchers provide their best estimate of whether "Basic Income Makes Sense,"[4] and they will tend to look for that answer in any report on the study. If they get no help doing it, they are likely to overestimate the political implications of the information that experiments find, providing a great opportunity for spin and sensationalism by people willing to seize on small findings that sound positive or negative as proof that the program has been proven to be a success or a failure. Some of my previous work has argued that earlier UBI-related experiments have been misunderstood and misused in these ways.[5] This book focuses mostly on how to avoid those problems.

Although so far, I have only talked about difficulties related to the science involved, ethical and moral issues complicate the issue even further. In terms of the analogy, this puzzle is a very special kind: the pieces fit together in different ways depending on one's moral values. In concrete terms, if a policy is sustainable, achieves some goal, and has some side effects, reasonable people can disagree about how good or bad those goals and side effects are and how we should evaluate tradeoffs between them. Except in the rare case where research definitively proves a policy has failed to achieve its supporters' goals, reasonable people can disagree on whether the evidence indicates the policy works and should it be introduced or if that same evidence indicates the policy does not work and should be rejected. This problem greatly affects the UBI discussion because supporters and opponents tend to take very different moral positions.

[4] Condliffe.
[5] Widerquist.

Many people, including many specialists, are less than fully aware of the extent to which their beliefs on policy issues are driven by empirical evidence about a policy's effects or by controversial moral evaluation of those effects. For example, mainstream economic methodology incorporates a money-based version of utilitarianism. Nonmoney-based utilitarianism was the prevailing ethical framework when basic mainstream economic techniques were developed, but it lost prominence decades ago. Many articles in economics journals read as if the author is unaware of the controversial moral judgments incorporated into that methodology.

Additionally, not everyone is honest about the extent to which their policy judgments are driven by controversial moral judgments. Some will try to spin the results by hiding the extent to which their evaluation of the evidence is driven by their moral position and portray it as the only objective reality. Specialists are not above exaggerating the definitiveness of their research.

Into this ethical morass falls the dense and difficult research report of an experiment's findings with an often tedious and easily ignorable list of caveats about the research's limitations and usually a complete absence of discussion about the moral judgments needed to evaluate the study's implications for policy. Under such circumstances, social science experiments easily fall victim to misunderstanding, spin, sensationalism, and oversimplification. Perhaps we should expect these problems to happen more often than not.

After all, it is easier to understand an oversimplification than genuine complexity.

Solutions to these problems are difficult and imperfect, but we have to try to address them, if UBI experiments are going to achieve their goal.

I presume the overall goal of UBI experiments is (and should be) to enlighten the public discussion by increasing the public understanding of evidence about UBI. I don't think that this goal is controversial or new. I believe it should be endorsed by virtually any UBI-related experiment, no matter what other goals it might have, such as the basic goal of scientific research (mentioned above), working out technical issues that are important to policymakers, or in some cases, politically promoting UBI. There is nothing inherently wrong with using a study—even a small-scale, less rigorous study—to promote a policy, as long as the evidence is presented honestly and aimed at improved understanding. Therefore, the need to keep the goal of enlightening discussion through good communication and an orientation toward the most important issues is as important to virtually all UBI studies.

Some past researchers (either conducting or writing about experiments) have failed to appreciate how difficult it is to accomplish this goal, especially when they focus primarily on the basic goal of scientific research. Increasing the amount of knowledge available to the scientific community does not necessarily or easily translate into improved public understanding of that evidence. The gap in background knowledge has to be addressed because it creates risks that less politically oriented research does not have, including vulnerability to misunderstanding, spin, misuse, sensationalism, or oversimplification.

Perhaps the main message of this book is that UBI experiments seldom, if ever, succeed in enlightening the public discussion merely by trying to get nonspecialists to understand experimental findings on their own terms. It's not enough to explain what the experimental group is, what a control group is, and what the differences were between the two groups in the study. It's not enough to have a new and improved list of caveats about experimental limitations.

Experimental findings should not be presented as a stand-alone piece of research but as a small part of a larger effort to use all available evidence to answer the big questions about UBI and to explain the extent to which the big questions remain unanswered. Researchers have to attempt to find the information that will be of most value to the public discussion, and someone—not necessarily the researchers conducting the study—has to attempt the difficult task of communicating those results in a way that people involved in the public discussion of the issue will understand. The difficulty of these tasks is at least half of what this book is about.

The book discusses the difficulty of conducting UBI experiments and communicating their results, given both the inherent limits of experimental techniques and the many barriers that make it difficult for researchers, journalists, policymakers, citizens, and anyone else interested in UBI or UBI experiments to understand each other. The book's goals are to improve both the experiments and the public understanding of them.

With the experiments' goal of enlightening the public discussion in mind, this book asks two distinct but closely related questions: (1) how do you do a good experiment given the difficulties involved? (2) How can citizens, policymakers, researchers, journalists, and others interested in UBI and UBI experiments communicate in ways that lead to a better public understanding of the experiments' implications for the public discussion of UBI? I am less interested in the question of whether we should have experiments, taking it for granted that they are happening, but that question will come up.

This project is an applied examination of a family of problems *specific* to UBI experiments, with no claim that these problems are necessarily ***unique*** to UBI experiments. Many such difficulties apply to all social science experiments, and some apply to all policy-related research.[6] To the best of my knowledge, this book is the first to focus entirely on applying this kind of analysis to UBI experiments, but it does not explore whether the kinds of problems discussed for UBI experiments are as bad or worse than the problems involved in other social science experiments.

This book is written for anyone interested in UBI experiments and UBI as a policy—that is, for researchers, journalists, policymakers, citizens, and people who are a little in one group and a little in another. Dangers of misunderstanding exist between everyone involved; everyone involved can help solve them; no single group can easily fix them on their own; and hopefully we can all benefit from thinking through the problems this book examines.

Policymakers, journalists, and citizens who understand the place of experiments in the political economy of the UBI discussion can better communicate their desire for experiments relevant to that discussion. They will learn more from whatever experiments are conducted. And they will be better prepared to counter spin and sensationalism.

Researchers who understand the place of experiments in the political economy of the UBI discussion can communicate their results more effectively. But it's not just about communication. Researchers who understand and respect the public discussion can design better experiments.

Researchers conducting experiments cannot resolve all these communication issues on their own. Although research specialists are professionals at communicating with other specialists, the vast majority of them are amateurs at communicating with nonspecialists—and I am no exception. Scientists are trained to conduct research and communicate it to other scientists, but have no special training in the skills needed to bridge the communication gap between them and nonspecialists. Very often specialists don't know what evidence would be most valuable to citizens or policymakers or how best to help citizens and policymakers understand the value of the evidence researchers are able to find.

[6] Similar work in other fields include Angus Deaton and Nancy Cartwright, "Understanding and Misunderstanding Randomized Controlled Trials," in *NBER Working Paper Series*, ed. National Bureau of Economic Research (Cambridge, MA: National Bureau of Economic Research, 2016); and Dawn Langan Teele, ed. *Field Experiments and Their Critics: Essays on the Uses and Abuses of Experimentation in the Social Sciences* (New Haven, CT: Yale University Press, 2014).

The ultimate responsibility rests more with the policymakers and donors *commissioning* experiments than with the researchers conducting experiments. They—or whoever they put in charge of hiring researchers to conduct experiments—are the ones with the most power to make sure the communication gaps are addressed.

With experiments getting underway and findings about to come out, it's important to consider lessons in how to improve the chances that experiments will successfully enlighten the public discussion of UBI. As the book argues, past UBI-related experiments—despite almost always being good science—have a mixed record at increasing the understanding of evidence among nonspecialists. Some succeeded and some failed.

The primary goal of a UBI experiment might simply be to examine a few narrow technical issues that are of particular interest to policymakers commissioning the study or to the research community. There is nothing wrong with the desire to make some goal like this the main focus of a project. But they ignore the public role of UBI experiments at their peril. UBI experiments are too closely tied to the political process and their results are too easily misunderstood for researchers to ignore experiments' role in the political economy of the UBI discussion without risking misuse and misunderstanding.

Although UBI experiments are scientific endeavors, they are both an outcome of and an input into the political process. The current experiments are—directly or indirectly—a response to the growth of the UBI movement. It is no coincidence that UBI-related experiments have taken place in two intervals (1968–1980 and 2008–the present) corresponding with waves of support for UBI and related policies.[7]

These enormous undertakings require great political support to come about. Social science experiments are usually too big to be funded by an everyday grant from a science foundation. The 1970s experiments were commissioned by acts of national legislatures that were seriously considering the policy. The same is true for the new government-funded experiments, such as those in Finland and Canada. Experiments in Namibia, India, Kenya, and two in the United States are all led or funded by private organizations with a strong interest in the UBI debate, although sometimes a mix of private and public institutional funding has been involved.

[7] Karl Widerquist, "Three Waves of Basic Income Support," in *Palgrave International Handbook of Basic Income*, ed. Malcolm Torry (New York: Palgrave Macmillan, Forthcoming).

Whether researchers like it or not, people on all sides of the UBI discussion all over the world will look to UBI experiments for information about UBI and sometimes for ammunition to use in debate. The experiments will affect the public discussion of UBI. People will seize on findings and say it implies X about whether UBI works or whether we should introduce it. The data will be used this way. The question is whether it will be understood and used appropriately or misunderstood and abused.

To achieve the goal of enlightening discussion, people commissioning and conducting experiments need to know the local discussion well, but they also need to avoid overconfidence in their belief about how well they know it. Journalists and opinion writers who have platforms to write about UBI are not necessarily experts on the UBI discussion. Major media outlets do not contain most of or even the most important parts of that discussion. People commissioning and conducting experiments should not be tempted to believe that no one in the local discussion is interested in the big questions that haven't been explicitly stressed by prominent writers and speakers involved in the discussion. Ignoring the obvious and rational desire for anyone considering a public policy question to have answers to the big questions about it creates an opportunity for a demagogue to use that lack of information to spin the experiment's findings to their advantage.

The limitations of UBI experiments, discussed throughout this book, might inspire some people to reject experiments altogether. This is not my message; the message instead is how best to conduct a UBI experiment and communicate its results once the decision to conduct an experiment is made. Experiments are happening; let's make them as good as possible.

The nature of this book requires me to say a little something about my perspective. I am an academic researcher. I have PhDs in Economics and Political Theory, but my job title is Associate Professor of Philosophy. I've supported UBI and related policies since 1980. I started writing about it in 1996 and publishing on it in 1999. I'm convinced by existing evidence that the advantages of UBI are so much greater than the disadvantages that most nations should introduce some form of it as soon as possible.

I also believe strongly in honest argument and evidence-based reasoning. Thus, I'm a committed supporter who tries also to be a dispassionate researcher. I have good knowledge of the topic, but I'm vulnerable to confirmation bias. Also, I might not always know whether I'm framing things in the most accurate way or in a way that spins them toward my existing beliefs. I'll try to take that into account as I write, and you should too as you read. I believe this book will be equally useful to people on all sides of the public discussion of UBI if readers look skeptically at my argument and evidence.

Although I bring a wide interdisciplinary perspective to this project (having written about UBI as a philosopher, an economist, a political theorist, an applied public policy researcher, and an amateur journalist), my experience is still far narrower than would be ideal for the effort at hand. I don't believe anyone could claim expertise in all the fields relevant to this book. UBI experiments cross all of the social sciences, many health sciences, as well as some technical fields like statistics, mathematics, and computer programming. To understand the political economy of the public discussion of UBI experiments, one would need practical experience across numerous countries in activism, journalism, science communication, grassroots organizing, political campaigns, and high-level public decision-making. And so, this book will necessarily delve into some topics that are beyond my expertise.

The book makes many specific recommendations, including strategies for conducting an effective test and for combatting spin and misunderstanding. Perhaps the best way to sum up my perspective is the following recommendation: **treat experiment(s) as a small part of the effort to answer the questions necessary to evaluate UBI as a policy proposal**. This recommendation does not mean that experiments must be conducted in conjunction with many other research efforts to answer all these questions. It means that experiments in isolation cannot be interpreted as saying very much at all about UBI as a policy. The true value of an experiment is making a small contribution to this larger effort. For nonspecialists to understand this: additional evidence has to be discussed, and the limits of experimental methods (and the overall effort to research a policy prior to implementation) have to be stressed.

In addition to many more specific suggestions, the book stresses four broad strategies to help experiments enlighten the discussion of UBI:

1. **Work back and forth from the public discussion to the experiment**. Anyone commissioning, conducting, or writing about experiments should respect the national or regional discussion of UBI. Find out what they can about what people most want to know. Design a study oriented as much as possible toward the questions that are important to the local discussion, with careful attention to the extent to which experiment can and cannot contribute to our understanding of those issues. All reports about experimental findings should relate the information to the big questions that are important to the local discussion. This strategy involves bringing in nonexperimental data and calling attention to the remaining, but it is necessary to help people appreciate the contribution an experiment can make.

2. **Focus on the effects rather than the side effects of UBI**. Research projects have a way of focusing attention on the things they can measure at the expense of more difficult questions that might be more important to the policy issue at hand. For example, past experiments have often focused on quantifiable self-effects, such as labor effort and cost at the expense of more important but less quantifiable issues, such as whether UBI has the positive effects on people's well-being as supporters predict.
3. **Focus on the bottom line**. Although the public discussion varies enormously over time and place, the desire for an answer to the big questions is ubiquitous, and so I suggest focusing on what I call the bottom line: an overall evaluation of UBI as a long-term, national policy.[8] Experiments alone cannot provide enough evidence to answer a bottom-line question, but researchers can relate all of their findings to it. Virtually all UBI research has some relevance to the bottom line, but citizens and policymakers often need a great deal of help understanding that relevance meaningfully. Even the best journalists are not always able to provide that help.
4. **Address the ethical controversy**. Researchers cannot resolve the controversy over the ethical evaluation of UBI, nor should they try. But they do the public a disservice by ignoring it. They can better head off spin by recognizing the controversy and explaining what the findings mean to people who hold different ethical positions that are common locally and perhaps internationally as well.

I wish I could say this strategy fully resolves the problem, but that isn't possible. A social science experiment is a very limited tool, and its implications are inherently difficult to understand. The effort to treat experiments as a small and incomplete part of a wider effort to answer all the important empirical issues about UBI will help but won't eliminate misunderstanding.

There will always be gaps in understanding between the people involved in the discussion of such a complex issue and such complex evidence. If a nonspecialist learns everything a specialist knows, they become a specialist. But experimentation and communication can always be improved. I hope this research project makes a small contribution to that effort.

[8] UBI can, of course, be a regional policy. This fact has not been repeated in the rest of the book to keep the language simple.

This book is organized in 19 chapters, beginning with this introduction.

Chapter 2 defines and explains the workings of UBI and its more easily testable cousin, the Negative Income Tax (NIT).

Chapter 3 discusses some necessary definitions and the pros and cons of the available testing techniques: randomized controlled trials (RCTs), saturation studies, and combinations of the two.

Chapter 4 discusses several general problems that virtually any UBI experiment will have to deal with: community effects, long-term effects, the Hawthorne effect, the streetlight effect, and the difficulty of separating the effects of the size and type of program being studied.

Chapter 5 discusses one big difficulty: the practical impossibility of testing UBI under most circumstances and the problems created by using NIT as an approximation of UBI.

Chapter 6 discusses the five NIT experiments conducted in the 1970s in the United States and Canada, summarizes their findings, and shows how badly they were misunderstood at the time. It argues that although the experiments succeeded in the scientific goal of obtaining useful data, they badly failed in the goal of enlightening the public discussion.

Chapter 7 discusses more recent findings from two experiments conducted in the late 2000s and early 2010s and from newly released data from one of the 1970s experiments, showing how these findings had a more positive impact on the public understanding of UBI.

Chapter 8 briefly discusses some of the now ongoing UBI experiments, proposed UBI experiments, and experiments in policies similar to UBI. The book references these experiments only rarely because its goal is not to analyze or criticize them, but to offer some useful analysis to the people commissioning, designing, conducting, reporting on, and reading about them.

Chapter 9 discusses the surprisingly complex political economy of the decision process that brings about UBI experiments in response to a movement more interested in the immediate introduction of UBI. It shows that experiments' vulnerability to misunderstanding and misuse make them a risky strategy for the UBI movement.

Chapter 10 examines why the results of experiments are so easily misunderstood, and therefore, vulnerable to misuse. These problems happen because of the inherent complexity of the material and the differences in background knowledge of the people involved.

Chapter 11 explains why UBI experiments cannot resolve the public disagreement about UBI. It argues that experiments can only make a small contribution to the large body of available evidence. The discussion turns less on remaining unknowns about UBI's effects than on the ethical desirability of UBI's known effects.

Chapter 12 begins the effort to work backward from the claims important to the public discussion of UBI to the claims experiments are able to examine. It suggests that UBI experiments should relate all findings to the bottom line, the overall cost-effectiveness of a fully implemented national UBI. An issue-specific bottom line for any variable of interest should also be considered.

Chapter 13 proposes a list of important empirical claims made by supporters and opponents of UBI in an effort to identify what empirical questions UBI experiments should focus on and how researchers can relate experimental findings to the things people really want to know about.

Chapter 14 identifies several empirical claims that should not be ignored but that cannot be tested on an experimental scale. Evidence about these claims will have to come from other sources, which will have to be combined with experimental evidence to connect it to the bottom line.

Chapter 15 identifies several claims that cannot be tested on an experimental scale but cannot be left out of the discussion of UBI's bottom line. It offers suggestions about how to treat them.

Chapter 16 discusses claims that can be examined by UBI tests, but shows that each of them can only be tested partially, indirectly, and/or inconclusively. It discusses the implications these limitations have for conducting a study and communicating its results.

Chapter 17 discusses possible ways to test UBI in light of these issues, working down from the dream test that solves all testing problems to tests that might be possible within the experiment's budget.

Chapter 18 considers whether it is after all worthwhile to have a UBI experiment, given all the difficulties tests have in addressing the most important issues in the public discussion.

Chapter 19 concludes with a discussion of how to work forward from the experimental results to the public discussion in ways that overcome communication barriers and reduce the problems associated with them. It argues that it is not enough to communicate the findings of experiments on their own terms, but results have to be presented with an understanding of the role they play in the political economy of the UBI discussion.

CHAPTER 2

Universal Basic Income and Its More Testable Sibling, the Negative Income Tax

Abstract This chapter defines and explains the workings of Universal Basic Income and its more easily testable cousin, the Negative Income Tax.

Keywords Basic income • Universal Basic Income • Unconditional basic income • Negative Income Tax • Basic Income Guarantee • Inequality • Poverty

UBI is commonly defined as a periodic, cash income paid individually to all members of a political community without means test or work requirement.[1] UBI is also commonly understood to be regular, stable in size, and lifelong, although it might be lower for children or higher for people of retirement age. This definition probably reflects the most common usage of the term, but UBI is a contested concept that is used differently in different political contexts and by different people in the same context.

Under this definition, every citizen of a nation (or every legal resident of a region) receives a regular income from the government (or some other authority) regardless of whether they have any other income, wealth, potential for employment, and so on.

[1] The Basic Income Earth Network defined UBI this way at its 2016 meeting in an effort to reflect common usage.

K. Widerquist, *A Critical Analysis of Basic Income Experiments for Researchers, Policymakers, and Citizens*, Exploring the Basic Income Guarantee, https://doi.org/10.1007/978-3-030-03849-6_2

Many of the claimed benefits of UBI depend on it being high enough to live on or even enough to live in dignity and social inclusion. If we want to test those claims, we need to test that level of UBI. Experiments have tended to focus on some conception of "enough," but not always one that all UBI supporters would agree is adequate.

Some people subtract the criteria that UBI is paid individually and without a means test. That is, a grant paid to a household and phased out as income rises. NIT is the more common name for a program that lacks those two criteria but otherwise guarantees a basic level of income. The second characteristic (that it is paid at the household level) follows from the first because most households pool their income and pay taxes as a unit.

Not everyone recognizes the distinction between NIT and UBI. For example, in Canada, the terms "basic income" and NIT are often used equivalently, and the NIT version under the name "basic income" currently dominates the discussion among policymakers, although that terminology is controversial among Canadian supporters.

The NIT is important to any discussion of UBI experiments because—as later chapters show—the differences between NIT and UBI make NIT more easily testable in an experiment.

That's all there is to UBI in the definitional sense, but it has an additional inherent feature necessary for its operation: UBI has to be financed with taxes or it will cause rampant inflation. Conceivably UBI could be financed by some enormous jointly owned asset, but in most political contexts, such an asset could not be created without introducing new taxes, and so this book focuses on the tax-financed model.

Any UBI system is defined by two essential parameters: the "grant" or "guarantee" level, which is simply the size of the UBI, and the "marginal tax rate" or "take-back rate," which is the rate at which taxes gradually become larger than the UBI. Any tax could be used to support UBI. Popular options include income tax, wealth tax, sales tax, and resource tax (i.e. taxes on the rental value of privately owned natural or socially created resources such as land, the broadcast spectrum, and the banking system). Given the need to finance UBI (or face rampant inflation), the actual financial benefit any individual gets from the UBI system is its *net* benefit—the difference between what one receives in UBI and what one pays in taxes.

The income-tax-financed UBI is not necessarily the most popular version of the program, but it simplifies the mathematics and is, therefore, popular with researchers conducting experiments.

NIT is similar enough to an income-tax-financed UBI that the same mathematical formulas can be used to show the net benefit of both. (I'll spare you the math.) The difference is that under UBI, the grant stays the same as taxes increase, while under NIT, taxes remain zero as the grant (i.e. the "negative tax") is gradually reduced to zero—at the breakeven point—and only then are taxes (i.e. "positive taxes") introduced.

For example, for a $12,000 UBI or NIT with a marginal tax rate of 50%, an individual making no private income receives a net income of $12,000. An individual making $12,000 receiving a net income of $18,000, and an individual with a net income at the "break-even point" of $24,000 receives a net income of $24,000. Their UBI is equal to the taxes they pay on their income.

Some people argue that NIT and UBI are effectively the same policy with insignificant administrative differences. But others argue that the differences are important. Some differences are purely administrative: NIT saves the trouble of paying a UBI to net contributors and taking it back from the same people in taxes, but UBI saves the trouble of determining who is eligible at a moment's notice when someone suddenly loses their income. Presumably, people will have to apply for an NIT and prove that their income has gone down before they receive it. This process could be difficult for people in a sudden economic crisis, such as a divorce, the loss of a job, or the failure of a business. No such issue exists with UBI. It would be directly deposited into one's account regardless of whether taxes were also coming out of one's paycheck. As an individual grant UBI might make it harder for one spouse to dominate the family's income.

Terms such as "Basic Income Guarantee" (BIG) and "Guaranteed Income" are sometimes used generically as terms for both UBI and NIT. BIG ensures that everyone has a nonzero income whether or not they have private income. Either form of BIG can be used to maintain the same minimum guarantee level for people who have no other income.

The controversial question among supporters is whether the seemingly small administrative differences between the two policies are significant enough that one model should be preferred over another. This is a question that one would ideally want to address in a test, but later chapters will show, tests usually have to focus on NIT.

Either form of BIG represents a fundamental break with the traditional social welfare strategy. Although welfare systems vary greatly in their level of generosity, virtually all of them require individuals to meet specific conditions to be eligible for the vast majority of their programs. Potential recipients must prove they are disabled to be eligible for one kind of program, unable to find a job to be eligible for another, injured to receive another, aged to receive another, working to receive another, and so on. Some programs, such as most countries' national health services, are universal and unconditional. BIG applies that unconditionality to large cash benefits.

UBI or NIT could replace a substantial portion of the existing welfare system. Exactly how many and which types of programs UBI could or should replace is a controversial question among supporters. A substantial UBI could most obviously replace income support for people with an ordinary level of need. It could not as easily replace additional income support for people with special greater needs, in-kind support for people who need special services, infrastructure, or public services (such as education and healthcare).

UBI needs to be tested in isolation. If researchers expose test UBI and some other policy (such as a new housing program) on the same people at the same time, their experiment won't reveal whether observed effects are attributable to UBI or to the other policy.

CHAPTER 3

Available Testing Techniques

Abstract This chapter discusses some necessary definitions and the pros and cons of the techniques available for field experiments of the Universal Basic Income. These techniques include randomized controlled trials, saturation studies, and combinations of the two.

Keywords Basic income experiments • Negative Income Tax experiments • Social science experiments • Basic income • Universal Basic Income • Randomized controlled trial • Saturation study • Saturation studies

After this chapter defines some relevant terms, it discusses the pros and cons of the techniques available for testing UBI.

All empirical research (whether experimental or not) attempts to answer a question appropriately called the research question. Often a large study, like a UBI experiment, will ask a series of research questions. A question like "what are UBI's effects" is too vague to be useful. A UBI could have an infinite number of effects, some important and some trivial. Although researchers would be happy to discover effects they were not looking for, you can't find an effect that you make no effort to measure.

K. Widerquist, *A Critical Analysis of Basic Income Experiments for Researchers, Policymakers, and Citizens*, Exploring the Basic Income Guarantee, https://doi.org/10.1007/978-3-030-03849-6_3

Most research questions are formulated around hypothesis testing. That is, they test a claim about a supposed relationship. For example, a lot of medical research tests the hypothesis that a medical treatment is safe.

Empirical studies seldom conclusively verify or falsify a claim. They can only state whether the evidence is consistent with or contradictory toward the claim, but this much is often extremely useful.

Sometimes there is little doubt that a treatment has a particular effect, and the research question becomes, "How large is that effect?" That sort of a research question is useful to examine, but to be a hypothesis test, it has to be paired with the claim that the effect is larger, smaller, or equal to some amount. For example, in wealthy countries, past evidence indicates UBI will correspond with a decline in the average time recipients spend in employment. The question is: how much it will decline? What size of a finding would be significant? Is it that the response is greater than zero? If so, we don't need a test. Is it that the response is greater than X%? If so, among which group? Is it that it is large enough to make the program unsustainable? Or is it something else entirely: perhaps the significance of this response is not in how large it is, but in some qualitative measure of what people do with the reduced time they spend working? The differences between these potential research questions create problems discussed in later chapters.

Two desirable attributes for estimates are that they are "accurate" and "unbiased." An accurate estimate is one that is likely to be close to the actual value. An "unbiased" estimate is one that is just as likely to overestimate the actual value as it is to underestimate it. That is, it lacks "statistical bias." Statistical bias is very different from the bias in the sense of favorability to one group over another.

Statistical bias cannot always be eliminated, and sometimes it has to be traded off against accuracy. A slightly biased estimation technique could be preferable to an unbiased but less accurate measure. For example, suppose you were estimating a person's age. A biased technique is likely to produce results anywhere from 1 year below to 2 years above their actual age. An unbiased technique is likely to produce an estimate anywhere from 20 years below to 20 years above their actual age. The accuracy of the biased technique almost certainly makes it more useful.

Bias causes great difficulty for empirical studies. Sometimes you don't know whether a technique is biased or not. Sometimes you know that it is likely to be biased, but you don't know which way. Sometimes you know that it is likely to be biased in a particular direction, but you don't know how much. All of these problems affect the testing of UBI.

One surprisingly controversial definitional issue is what to call the effort to try out UBI on a small scale to learn something about it in advance of full implementation. In common English, the words "test," "trial," "pilot," and "experiment" all fit that definition, but some of them are also used in more specific senses in technical settings.

"Experiment" is sometimes used to refer only to a "randomized controlled trial" (RCT): a test designed to isolate the effects of the factors being studied by using randomization as a method to control as much as possible for all other factors that might influence the relevant outcomes. Researchers do so by randomly selecting two sufficiently large groups that differ as little as possible from each other and from the wider population. They give the treatment to one group only (the experimental group) and observe whether that group differs in relevant ways from the other group (the control group). If the groups are sufficiently large and properly selected, the differences between them—other than those caused by the treatment—will tend to cancel each other out. This method is indispensable in many forms of medical research, and it can be useful in social science as well. But as argued below, it is not always the best way to address questions at issue in the UBI debate.

"Pilot" or "pilot project" can be used as a broader alternative to "experiment," but it carries baggage as well. "Pilot project" sometimes implies that the test is conducted by an authority with the power to fully implement the policy—at least if the pilot meets some criteria of success. Sometimes it implies that a firm decision in favor of full implementation has already been made, and the test is being used to determine *how* rather than whether to implement it.

Even the simple word "test" sometimes implies that the study involves some firm criteria by which the policy will be judged to have passed or failed. Nonspecialists often expect such criteria from experiments of any kind. Social science experiments are usually conducted without any criteria of success in mind in a context where success criteria are politically controversial debates. Therefore, it's best to fight the impression they have any such criteria.

The term "trial" or "implementation trial" has the fewest other connotations, and so I occasionally use it for clarity, but it is also the least familiar of these terms.

I mostly use the term "experiment" in that broader sense defined in the first paragraph of this chapter, despite how, as explained below, at least some specialists assert the common usage is wrong.

What distinguishes an experiment, test, trial, or pilot in this broad sense from a nonexperiment is that an experiment is in place solely (or at least primarily) to learn something about a potential policy. It is not (primarily) an attempt to *implement* the policy. In this sense, the NIT experiments of the 1970s were experiments, but the Alaska Dividend and Cherokee per capita payments, for example, are not.[1] Although these policies might provide a useful opportunity to learn something about UBI, they are not put in place for that opportunity.

Once the decision is made to conduct an experiment, researchers have a choice of two broad types of techniques or a combination of the two. The first, an RCT, is defined above. The second, a "saturation study," involves identifying two relevant communities, such as two small towns, and giving the treatment to everyone in one community and not to people in the other. Although researchers might randomly choose which of the two sites will be the control and which the experimental site, that level of randomness is not enough to control for other factors that might make one site different from another. Although the communities could be selected to be as similar to each other and to the wider population in as many observed ways as possible, they might differ in important but unobserved ways.

Both RCTs and saturation studies are useful. RCTs are better at examining issues in which most of the effects occur at the individual level. Though far from perfect, saturation studies are better at examining issues in which many important effects occur at the community level. These "community effects" are extremely important for UBI because its effects depend on the interactions of people in markets and cultural settings (see discussion below).

Whether the trial is an RCT or a saturation study, the experimental and control groups each need to be at least a few hundred (and preferably a few thousand people) to produce statistically useful results. How large the sample has to be depends on "the law of large numbers," a statistical principle stating that as the number of observations increases in an unbiased sample, the probability of the expected accuracy of that sample increases.

[1] Karl Widerquist and Michael W. Howard, eds., *Alaska's Permanent Fund Dividend: Examining Its Suitability as a Model* (New York: Palgrave Macmillan, 2012), *Exporting the Alaska Model: Adapting the Permanent Fund Dividend for Reform around the World* (New York: Palgrave Macmillan, 2012).

The law of large numbers begins to kick in between 20 and 30 observations, and for most purposes, 50 observations is enough to provide a high likelihood that the results should be highly accurate.

That makes UBI experiments sound affordable, but suppose you want results for men and women. Now you need 100 observations. Suppose you need a statistically useful sample of children, and people of various ethnic and religious groups. Now you need several hundred observations. Suppose you want to observe the effects of UBI on unemployment or pregnancy. Now you need well into the thousands, so that the number of people who become pregnant or employed during the study is statistically significant. Although a UBI experiment with a few hundred participants can produce useful results for some issues, most experiments usually try to get funding for a sample well into the thousands to examine more issues.

In wealthier countries, a sample of a few thousand people receiving a meaningfully large UBI is extremely expensive. But in less wealthy countries, where people live off extremely small incomes, much larger sample sizes are possible—perhaps into the tens of thousands. Thus, doing different kinds of experiments in different places is extremely useful.

Once the experimental group is selected and begins receiving "the treatment," researchers observe how they behave in comparison to the control group. The central goal of any experiment is to find a way to ensure differences between the two groups will be attributable as much as possible to the treatment and to random fluctuations, which tend to cancel out in a large enough sample. Hence the *control* in the experiment. Unfortunately, in social science, creating a trial that is both controlled and representative of how the policy under investigation will work under full implementation is extremely difficult.

Some researchers—labeled "Randomistas" by their critics—insist that only RCTs are truly scientific or truly deserving of the term "experiment."[2] One reason to resist the Randomista use of "experiment" is to avoid confusion caused by the belief that more technical definitions are the "right" definitions. That is not how language works. Specialists do not own the language or any terms within it. The most commonly used definition is the most acceptable definition. Specialists who insist that technical definitions

[2] Guy Standing, "Basic Income Pilot Schemes: Seventeen Design and Evaluation Imperatives," in *Wege Zum Grundeinkommen [Pathways to Basic Income]*, ed. D. Jacobi and W. Strengmann-Kuhn (Berlin: Bildungswerk Berlin, 2012).

are the only right definitions risk confusing nonspecialists, who are most familiar with the common understanding of "experiment" and who are important consumers of the findings of UBI experiments—or any policy-related experiment.

Another reason to resist the Randomista use of the word is that RCTs are not accurately described as the only scientific form of experiment.[3] RCTs make some valuable statistical techniques available that aren't available with saturation studies, and they make it possible to control for unobserved factors that saturation studies cannot control for. But they do so by entirely ignoring certain kinds of effects (discussed below). In other words, RCTs control for more things but test fewer things. Therefore, researchers should be open to using both RCTs and saturation studies as appropriate. Both techniques should be considered part of the social scientists' toolkit as long as researchers are careful to note the extent to which their results should be seen as tentative or conclusive and the ways in which those results are likely to be biased.

Each technique has some advantages over the other in each of these respects: important effects of UBI occur at both the individual and the community level. Individuals immediately react to UBI in many important ways that are worth estimating, but they interact with other individuals in markets, society, culture, and politics. All of these interactions generate important feedback effects throughout the community. Existing theory and empirical evidence indicate that some community effects might be as important or more important than the initial individual effects of UBI. If researchers opt only for an RCT they must choose between ignoring feedback effects entirely or supplementing their experimental data with information from other sources to simulate feedback. Guy Standing argues that the Randomista attitude often leads to ignoring community effects even on issues—such as UBI—where such effects are likely to be extremely important.[4]

Because both types of experiments have advantages and disadvantages, an ideal test would fully combine saturation and RCT techniques by randomly selecting dozens of saturation sites for both the control and experimental groups. For example, consider a test of whether a vaccine creates "herd immunity," which refers to the way a large number of individuals

[3] Andrew Gelman, "Experimental Reasoning in Social Science," in *Field Experiments and Their Critics: Essays on the Uses and Abuses of Experimentation in the Social Sciences*, ed. Dawn Langan Teele (New Haven, CT: Yale University Press, 2014).

[4] Standing.

with immunity in a group helps protect individuals without it. The individual immunity question can be answered by a simple RCT with a few hundred or a few thousand individual subjects, but the herd immunity question requires testing multiple herds. The effort becomes more difficult if we need to test how large or isolated the herd must be to establish herd immunity. These questions might require dozens or even hundreds of herds of varying sizes and levels of isolation to get statistically significant results. For herds of livestock, such a test might be affordable. For herds of humans, it is likely probably unaffordable.

Researchers have conducted experiments with multiple saturation sites in India and Kenya, where poverty is extremely high and a UBI of a dollar a day or less is extremely significant to recipients. The Kenyan study has the budget for a statistically significant number of saturation sites, but each site is too small to capture all of the relevant community effects, many of which probably occur at the national level.

Most likely, in wealthier countries, the techniques available will be limited to one RCT or one saturation site, or at best one of each.

CHAPTER 4

Testing Difficulties

Abstract This chapter discusses several general problems that virtually any experiment in the Universal Basic Income will have to deal with: community effects, long-term effects, the Hawthorne effect, the streetlight effect, and the difficulty of separating the effects of the size and type of program being studied.

Keywords Basic income experiments • Negative Income Tax experiments • Social science experiments • Basic income • Universal Basic Income • Community effects • Feedback effects • Hawthorne effect • Streetlight effect

This chapter discusses several difficulties that are likely to affect any UBI experiment and possible ways of dealing with each one, including community effects, the Hawthorne effect, the streetlight effect, and the difficulty of separating the effects of the size and type of policy being studied.

1 Community Effects

Community effects (defined in Chap. 3) will probably have a large impact on many, if not most, of the responses to UBI. This section explains why these effects create enormous difficulties for UBI experiments and makes some tentative suggestions about how to deal with them.

K. Widerquist, *A Critical Analysis of Basic Income Experiments for Researchers, Policymakers, and Citizens*, Exploring the Basic Income Guarantee, https://doi.org/10.1007/978-3-030-03849-6_4

Community effects are easiest to grasp when they work in the same direction as individual effects. For example, evidence indicates that inequality and the ghettoization of poverty exacerbate problems like ill-health, crime, poor education, and so forth, and sometimes inequality makes these problems worse even for the people who materially benefit from inequality.[1] If an individualized RCT finds that UBI has a positive effect on childhood health at the individual level, we can imagine that the effect will be even larger at the national level.

Community effects are more difficult to grasp when they (fully or partially) counteract individual effects. In such cases, the national effect might be much smaller or even the reverse of the more easily observable individual effects. For example, some obvious and important community effects of UBI have to do with the feedback effects between workers and employers, most particularly the labor demand response. Workers (at least in wealthier nations) are likely to respond to UBI by working less. Employers are likely to respond to that action by offering better wages and working conditions. Workers are likely to respond to better wages and working conditions by working more, partially counteracting their initial drop in hours worked. Call that a feedback loop. It involves the supply and demand for labor and for related goods. Many researchers have criticized RCTs—and all field experiments—for their inability to examine general equilibrium effects,[2] which are important not just to wages, working conditions, and working hours, but to all economic variables.

Culture, education, and other factors are likely to respond to those changes in the labor market, and these factors could feedback to other labor market changes. That feedback loop now has five potential steps. An RCT can measure only the first step in the six steps in that predicted loop. A saturation study might capture some of the second and third steps, but only to the extent that these effects occur at the local level. Therefore, an experiment will tell us very little about what we want to know about hours worked, wages, and the incomes of workers. All of these factors will have an important effect on the cost of UBI.

[1] Richard G. Wilkinson and Kate Pickett, *The Spirit Level: Why More Equal Societies Almost Always Do Better* (London: Allen Lane, 2009).

[2] Angus Deaton, "Instruments, Randomization, and Learning About Development," in *Field Experiments and Their Critics: Essays on the Uses and Abuses of Experimentation in the Social Sciences*, ed. Dawn Langan Teele (New Haven, CT: Yale University Press, 2014), p. 177; Philippe Van Parijs and Yannick Vanderborght, *Basic Income: A Radical Proposal for a Free Society and a Sane Economy* (Harvard University Press, 2017), p. 143.

Ideally, the extent to which feedback loops cause these effects is something we would like to investigate in an experiment. To do so, we would need a prohibitively expensive version of the herd immunity test described in Chap. 3. Many the of relevant community effects will be observable only at the national level, but a saturation study might pick up enough of them to be useful.

Researchers with limited budgets have at least four options for dealing with community effects. Each of them has a serious downside. First, conduct an RCT only and ignore community effects entirely: concentrate on explaining the difference in behavior between the control and experimental groups without concern for (an accurate) national prediction. This option, clearly the worst of the four, biases the results, sometimes in unpredictable ways, and even if the direction of bias is predictable, the size of the bias seldom is.

Second, conduct an RCT only, leaving all the biases in place, but include caveats explaining those biases. This option is likely to be popular with researchers, but it has many shortcomings. Specialists often have difficulty explaining caveats in ways nonspecialists can understand in the time they have. Readers often ignore them because they are usually tedious and difficult to understand. Caveats often get lost in the chain of communication connecting specialists to citizens and policymakers. In practice, this second option might not be that different from the first. The 1970s US experiments attempted this option, but as Chap. 6 shows, the public discussion proceeded with little or no recognition that unobservable community effects existed.

Third, conduct an RCT in combination with computer simulation analysis using theory and data from other sources to estimate community effects. This option means the report on the experimental findings will be driven less by those findings and more by the assumptions of that simulation model. Hopefully, the assumptions of those simulation models will be drawn from very good evidence, but evidence to the quality we want is seldom available.

Fourth, conduct a saturation study on at least one site (more if budget allows), combined (if budget allows) with an individualized RCT at another site or across a wide geographical area. Small, isolated communities are likely to have community effects more similar to those we can expect at the national level. For example, if the saturation site is fairly isolated, local businesses have to draw labor from potential employees who are all eligible for UBI rather than from nearby neighborhoods that are not involved in the study. Unfortunately, labor markets, even in isolated communities, are in many ways national and so even a saturation study is likely to be biased toward underestimating employer response, but they are an improvement on RCTs, which are unable to estimate employer responses at all. A saturation study won't provide evidence about how similar the community effects at the saturation site are to the community effects of a national program. Additionally, individuals in smaller, more isolated communities might not be representative of the people in larger, less isolated communities, where the majority of the world's population lives. This imperfect representativeness will bias the study in unknown ways.

2 The Hawthorne Effect

The "Hawthorne effect" is the problem of people changing their behavior when being observed. People in an experiment know they're being observed, and this knowledge might affect their behavior in unpredictable ways, causing many different forms of bias. Perhaps seeking approval of the observers, participants would behave in ways they think will make them look good or smart or successful to the observers. Perhaps instead they would show off, trying to be funny or interesting or trying to cultivate some kind of image. Perhaps they would try to "help" the observer by displaying what they think the observer wants to see. Perhaps they would try to "harm" the observer by displaying the opposite of what they think the observer wants to see, possibly because of some antagonistic feelings toward either the researcher or the research objective. Perhaps they would be affected by the power of suggestion: knowing that the observer wants to know whether they do X might unconsciously make them do X or make them avoid doing X more than they normally would. These reactions might sound silly, but no one can claim to be completely free of them. Hawthorne effects have been recognized for decades, but exactly how they are likely to affect research remains a mystery,[3] making it very difficult to compensate for them. One strategy is to observe people in an unobtrusive way for a long period of time in hopes that they gradually stop paying attention to their observers, but this strategy's success rate is hard to gage.

Hawthorne effects are likely to be a bigger problem for the new round of UBI experiments than they were in the 1970s. Today, most people post

[3] Jim McCambridge, John Witton, and Diana R. Elbourne, "Systematic Review of the Hawthorne Effect: New Concepts Are Needed to Study Research Participation Effects," *Journal of Clinical Epidemiology* 67, no. 3 (2014).

about themselves on social media, and it will be difficult to get them to avoid posting about a trial they are participating in. This visibility will make it easier for the media to find them, and the more attention they receive for participating in a study, the greater the Hawthorne effect is likely to be.

Saturation studies are more vulnerable to the Hawthorne effect than RCTs. A saturation site cannot be kept secret. Participants might have journalists, bloggers, activists, and long-lost friends contacting them to ask what it's like to be in the UBI saturation study.[4] How this increased attention will affect their behavior is unknown. I hope the problem does not make it impossible to do saturation studies in well-wired countries, but it might.

3 Long-Term Effects

Any experiment is going to be short term compared to how long the actual policy is likely to stay in place, and short-term effects often differ significantly from long-term effects. This problem is intuitively easy to grasp for people with no special training, but its magnitude is so great that it might create problems for understanding research. In most cases, the experimental UBI will be in place for only 2–4 years, while an actual UBI will be in place permanently, and we most want to understand its final, overall, long-term effects.

The effects of UBI on health, education, labor time, wages, working conditions, and so on are likely to involve community effects that develop out of economic and cultural interactions between people over a very long period. Experiments directly observe only the initial steps in that long, complex chain of reactions. Although some long-term effects are likely (at least) to be in the same direction as short-term effects, other long-term effects might partially or fully reverse the short-term effects. Following up with participants 5, 10, or 20 years after a temporary study has been completed is useful to see whether it has had lingering effects, but the lingering effects of a temporary policy are very different from the long-term effects of a policy that continues in place for 20 or more years. For example, some evidence indicates that the British labor force took as long as 70 or 80 years to react fully to the introduction of that nation's pension system.[5]

[4] Thanks to Evelyn Forget for alerting me to this last issue.

[5] Paul Johnson, "Parallel Histories of Retirement in Modern Britain," in *Old Age from Antiquity to Post-Modernity*, ed. Paul Johnson and Pat Thane (London: Routledge, 1998); http://blog.spicker.uk/experiments-with-basic-income-were-never-going-to-settle-the-arguments/

Researchers can try running a longer-term experiment, but doing so increases the expense and the time it takes to get results, and so most studies are very short term. The Seattle/Denver Income Maintenance Experiment (SIME/DIME) study contained the longest-run observations so far. It was originally planned for 6 years. After about 3 years, researchers obtained permission to extend the experiment to 20 years for a small subsample, but that effort was cancelled after 9 years.[6] That is, a small group was eligible for an NIT for 9 years, about six of which they were led to believe they would receive the NIT for 20 years. Researchers did not find major differences between this group and the shorter-term sample, but this RCT had no way to measure community effects, which are likely to be larger in the long run. How differently a national UBI would affect people over the long term still remains questionable. The best we can do is to extrapolate based on theory and data from other sources, imposing yet more assumptions about things we would rather like to learn from an experiment.

4 The Streetlight Effect

Although the "streetlight effect" is easy to understand, it might be the most difficult problem for experiments to avoid.

The streetlight effect gets its name from a joke in which a man loses his keys in a dark alley but looks for them under a streetlight because, he explains, "the light is so much better here." In social science, the "streetlight effect" is research that focuses on questions that are easier to answer but less important rather than on questions that are more important but harder to answer.

Few, if any, research techniques can examine all questions we have about a policy. Any study using any one technique draws attention to the questions that technique is better able to address and distracts attention from other, possibly more important questions.[7]

[6] P.K. Robins, "The Labor Supply Response of Twenty-Year Families in the Denver Income Maintenance Experiment," *Review of Economics and Statistics* 66, no. 3 (1984); Widerquist, "A Failure to Communicate: What (If Anything) Can We Learn from the Negative Income Tax Experiments?"

[7] Dawn Langan Teele, "Introduction," in *Field Experiments and Their Critics: Essays on the Uses and Abuses of Experimentation in the Social Sciences*, ed. Dawn Langan Teele (New

A social science experiment is a tool to help evaluate a potential policy. What's ultimately important about an experiment is its ability to do that. But an experiment is also a very specific tool that is much better at addressing some questions than others. Even the questions it can address, it can address only partially and/or indirectly—thereby producing information that is substantively different and possibly distracting from the most important information for the evaluation of that policy.

Experiments will find useful evidence, but understanding its value requires remaining focused on the big, evaluative questions and making the difficult, sometimes tenuous connection between that evidence and the important questions.

But research reports, academic literature, and popular literature on past experiments have overwhelmingly focused on the things experiments were best able to observe—differences between the control and experimental groups—as if those differences were the most important issues in evaluating UBI, or as if understanding those differences could be straightforwardly extrapolated into an understanding of the probable effects of policy introduced on a national scale.

Researchers usually include caveats about those limitations, but a list of caveats falls far short of a discussion of how the information found relates to the most important questions to ask in evaluating the potential for national adoption of a UBI program.

The potential for the streetlight effect plays a large role when this book considers which questions in the UBI discussion experiments can and cannot address.

5 The Difficulty of Separating the Effects of the Size from the Effects of the Type of Policy Being Studied

If implemented as most supporters envision, UBI involves both a large change in social welfare *strategy* and a large increase in social welfare *spending*. If we want an experiment to help us understand how UBI differs from other strategies, we need to separate the effects of the size from the effects of the type of program being studied.

Haven, CT: Yale University Press, 2014); Angus Deaton, "Instruments, Randomization, and Learning About Development," ibid.

Separating the effects of size and type is extremely difficult in a UBI experiment. The experiments in the United States in the 1970s tested various sizes of NIT, but they only had one control group, all the members of which were eligible for the welfare system existing at the time (see Chap. 6). Thus, the effects of the larger NITs were compared to the effects of the existing system and to smaller NITs, but not to equally generous versions of the existing system. This method gave some information about how the effects of NIT differ by size and some idea about how the effects of NIT differed from the effects of the existing system, but it could not determine the extent to which the effects of the larger NITs had more to do with their being larger or more to do with their being NITs rather than just a more generous version of the existing system.

Furthermore, most reports of results (including those summarized in Chap. 6) lumped together the findings from various experimental groups with various grant levels and marginal tax rates. This amalgamation not only made it difficult to separate the effects of size and type, but also made it difficult to interpret just what size of UBI was being tested on average. What then do the numbers say about the choice between introducing a generous UBI or using the same amount of money to make the existing system more generous or to introduce some other strategy? Unfortunately, it is difficult to extrapolate an answer from the experimental evidence. And that question is far closer to what people most want to know than whether the control group behaves differently from the experimental group. There are two ways to get the estimates closer to what we really want to know.

The first option is to include several different control groups facing differently generous versions of the existing system or whatever system UBI is being tested against. This might seem easy, but to get a really good estimate of the different effects of size and type of spending, each version of UBI would have to be paired with a different strategy of exactly the same size.

Unfortunately, for two so different strategies, it's difficult to determine in advance what size is the same. The cost of a public policy depends on overhead costs, take-up rate, and other factors, most of which can't be estimated in an experiment. Researchers can use data from other sources to estimate what an equal-sized version of the existing system might be. Although any estimate will be highly approximate, just having various sizes for the control groups will help tease out the difference between size and type.

However, none of the NIT or UBI experiments conducted so far have used this technique, and I don't expect any of the currently-under-discussion experiments will either, for one simple reason. It's expensive. It roughly doubles the cost of the experiment. Researchers will have to give out twice as many checks each week, and they will have to deal with the difficult administrative challenge of determining how much each individual in the control group would be eligible for this week if programs A, B, C, and D were X% more generous. They will have to somehow make up the difference, which is probably difficult enough for cash benefits, and extremely difficult for in-kind benefits such as public housing or food stamps.

The second option for examining the difference between size and type is to use theory and data from elsewhere in computer simulations to estimate how the control group would have responded to a more generous version of the existing system and use that as the baseline for comparison or at least as a way to estimate what portions of each observed difference between the control and experimental group are attributable to size or type. This method would also be highly approximate, but nevertheless, it is a potentially useful check on the simple comparison.

I don't know of any literature on past experiments that attempted to use this method. It was not emphasized in the discussion of any NIT or UBI experiment completed so far. Instead most of the literature reported the observed differences between the control group and the experimental group, mentioning what the two groups were eligible for, and sometimes with no further explanation at all, leaving it up to readers to understand that the results, therefore, involve some amalgamation of the effects of the size and type of plan being studied. The popular literature at the time shows little or no awareness of this issue.

The two methods of accounting for the difference between size and type are expensive or difficult or not necessarily very accurate or a mix of all three. Simply explaining the issue takes some effort and all it does is leave readers with the possibly disappointing realization that the numbers are less meaningful than they might initially have appeared to be.

CHAPTER 5

The Practical Impossibility of Testing UBI

Abstract This chapter discusses one big difficulty with conducting experiments in Universal Basic Income (UBI): the practical impossibility of testing it under most practical circumstances and the problems created by using the Negative Income Tax as an approximation of UBI.

Keywords Basic income experiments • Negative Income Tax experiments • Social science experiments • Basic income • Universal Basic Income • Negative Income Tax • Inequality • Poverty

This chapter makes two arguments. First, in wealthy countries, it is effectively impossible to test UBI in practice: an experiment either tests something else (usually NIT) instead of UBI or tests a UBI plus an influx of money that would not normally accompany UBI, making the test unrepresentative in other important ways. Second, at best, a test examines half of the effects of UBI or NIT because no test can include the effect of taxes on net contributors to the UBI program. These problems don't mean researchers should give up; experiments can test NIT as an approximation of UBI and attempt to look at net recipients in isolation, but understanding and accounting for the biases created by these substitutions is not easy.

K. Widerquist, *A Critical Analysis of Basic Income Experiments for Researchers, Policymakers, and Citizens*, Exploring the Basic Income Guarantee, https://doi.org/10.1007/978-3-030-03849-6_5

1 Forces Pushing Tests Toward NIT

Simulating UBI in a trial might deceptively seem simple: randomly select people and give them a UBI. But the UBI grant is not all there is to a UBI program. It requires taxes, or it will cause rampant inflation. Although everyone gets the UBI, the vast majority of people in wealthy countries also pay at least some taxes. And, although the size of UBI is the same for everyone, the net benefit individuals receive varies with the amount of taxes they pay. The net benefit is what affects their available choices, not the nominal amount of the grant. And—except in the poorer and more unequal countries—almost everyone can be expected to pay at least some taxes, so that very few people will receive a net benefit equal to the full amount of the grant, and the average net benefit might be much less than the full grant.

It is easy to give a UBI grant to a group of people. It is difficult to get the right net benefit to each of them—at least not in the *way* a true UBI system gets the net benefit to people. This difficulty arises because researchers can't levy special taxes on participants in an experiment. Researchers have at least three options for dealing with this problem.

The first option is to include in the study only people who would pay little or no taxes under the UBI program being examined. The difference between this group's gross and net benefit from the UBI will be zero or negligible. This solution can work in less wealthy, more unequal countries that have extreme inequality and a large number of very poor people who pay no taxes now and would not need to start paying taxes to finance a significant UBI. The Namibian and Indian experiments studied very impoverished villages where few, if any, of the residents would pay any taxes at all under a full-fledged UBI system.

However, in wealthy nations, very few people pay zero taxes now, and even fewer would pay no (gross) taxes under most proposed UBI schemes. Under a reasonably affordable version of UBI, people would probably have to start paying taxes from a very low income or even from the first dollar of income,[1] so that their net benefit gradually declines as income rises at a rate that will reach a reasonably affordable break-even point. The taxes don't have to be income taxes, but the tax has to fall partly on net

[1] Anthony Atkinson, *Public Economics in Action: The Basic Income/Flat Tax Proposal* (Oxford: Clarendon Press, 1995); Karl Widerquist, "The Cost of Basic Income: Back-of-the-Envelope Calculations," *Basic Income Studies* 12, no. 2 (2017).

recipients to ensure affordability. Under such a UBI scheme, most people would enter the no-tax-paying group for no more than a few months at a time, and researchers could not predict in advance who would be most likely to remain in that group longest unless they focused on the disabled—which would defeat the purpose of testing unconditional basic income. Therefore, UBI experiments in wealthy nations simply cannot focus on people for whom the difference between gross and net benefit is zero or negligible.

The second option would be to ignore the difference between gross and net benefit, even though it is non-negligible. This option enormously exaggerates the effects of UBI. The typical net beneficiary in a reasonably-affordable-but-adequate-sized UBI is likely to live in a household that makes substantial private income and benefits by less than half the nominal amount of the UBI, depending on many specific factors about the size and method of financing of the UBI.[2] Ignoring this difference would render any observations of participants' behavior almost meaningless as a prediction of what they would do under an actual UBI system.

Furthermore, the *rate* at which participants' net benefit decreases as they make more money (or do other things that might increase their tax burden under various possible financing regimes) is likely to have an important effect on their decision-making and behavior. It simply can't be ignored if the results of the test are going to be at all useful in estimating the effects of a real UBI. Therefore, any reasonable UBI experiment has to focus on the net rather than gross benefit, but as mentioned above, researchers can't levy taxes.

The third option is to simulate new taxes by reducing participants' grant as their income goes up. But as Chap. 3 mentioned, a grant that goes down as income goes up is not a UBI; it's an NIT.

An NIT scheme can create the same after-tax distribution of income as a UBI scheme that happens to have the same marginal income tax rate, and so it is reasonable to say that NIT is a good proxy for UBI in an experiment. But, as Chap. 2 explained, NIT works differently in some important ways. The practical effects of the differences between NIT and UBI are controversial among people who study or advocate for various forms of BIG. We would ideally like to test these differences in an experiment. Instead, experiments will have to assume that these differences are small enough to use an NIT as an approximation of UBI.

[2] "The Cost of Basic Income: Back-of-the-Envelope Calculations."

Using NIT to approximate UBI forces the experiment to employ at least a partially income-tax-financed UBI. From the 1960s to the 1990s, the USBIG discussion was dominated by the income-tax-financed version.[3] But this version is no longer central to the discussion. Many recent proposals focus on rent and resource taxes, banking reforms, wealth taxes, and so on as methods of financing UBI. Many such taxes do not fall directly on net beneficiaries of UBI, but might or might not be passed onto them through the market—once again the kind of thing we would like to test in an experiment rather than to impose on an experiment by assumption.

However, the flat income tax in an experiment has a lot of advantages. It makes the math extremely easy, and whatever type of tax is used, the amount of taxes people end up paying is likely to be heavily correlated with income, so an experiment can use the flat tax as an approximation for any other tax, hopefully without too much loss of generality.

UBI experiments will also be forced to take on the second characteristic of NIT: they will have to give the grant on a household basis rather than an individual basis. Researchers can't simply select a group of individuals at random and give them each a UBI because most of those individuals live in households and the effect of UBI on one person in a household where everybody gets a UBI is very different from the effect of a UBI on one person in a household where no one else gets one. Therefore, RCTs will have to draw households at random rather than individuals at random, and they will have to assume doing so does not affect observed behavior.

Furthermore, because most people pay taxes as households, researchers will have to treat those households as a unit, reducing every household member's UBI to simulate the increase in taxes as one member's income goes up, effectively making the UBI a household grant rather than an individual grant. For example, imagine a household where only the father receives a private income. A UBI gives a separate income to father, mother, and child, while all of the family's income taxes come out of the father's income. Suppose the father's income rises. Under a fully implemented UBI system, everyone's separate UBI grant stays the same, while the father pays more taxes. Under the experimental NIT system, the one NIT grant check they receive as a household unit goes down to simulate the new taxes on the father's larger income. The overall effect on the house-

[3] Atkinson.

hold's income as a whole is exactly the same. Does this mean that they react the same? We don't actually know. It depends on whether receiving separate UBIs affects the distribution of spending within the household—again the sort of question we'd like to learn from an experiment. Because we are forced to use an NIT as a proxy for UBI, researchers will have to assume that the family will react exactly the same whether the grant is individual or household based.

2 Testing Half the Effects

No UBI or NIT experiment can test the effects of BIG on net contributors—people who pay more taxes than they receive in UBI. No one would volunteer for a trial that substantially reduced their income, and forced participation is ethically and legally problematic. Probably all we can do is ignore the effect on net contributors. Unfortunately, for a program as large and costly as UBI, the effects on net beneficiaries can't be isolated from the effects on net contributors, causing at least four problems.

First, some people's income moves back and forth across the break-even point, changing their status from net recipient to net contributor. Leaving out the additional taxes they pay as net contributors exaggerates both the financial incentive to earn more private income and the size of this group's income over time. There is a good chance that the marginal effect of these taxes will be small enough to ignore, but once again, that is something we would ideally like to learn from an experiment.

Second, net beneficiaries interact in the market and elsewhere with net contributors. Feedback loops will be substantial because, assuming balanced-budget financing, as much money comes out of the economy from net contributors as goes into it via net beneficiaries. The same amount of money is likely to have a smaller effect on the behavior of net contributors than of net recipients. Researchers can use data from other sources to estimate the likely effects on net contributors. There is a wealth of data on how taxation affects behavior. Researchers can then use computer simulations to estimate the feedback effects. Not much of the literature on the 1970s NIT experiments involved these kinds of simulations.[4] And once again, the assumptions of the simulation are things we would ideally like to test in an experiment.

[4] See Chap. 6.

Third, even saturation studies will be unable to examine the effects of taxes on net contributors. In a wealthy country, representative saturation sites will have substantial numbers of both net contributors and net beneficiaries. Because the study reflects the larger budgets of net recipients but ignores the smaller budgets of net contributors, it will exaggerate the effect of UBI on the economic activity of the community as a whole. This imbalance is likely to exaggerate economic activity in the community and therefore exaggerate the opportunities available to net recipients. Again, the effect might be small, but it is another assumption to impose on the experiment and another caveat to explain.

Fourth, in practical terms, the largest problem with the inability to include net contributors might not be one of biasing the results, but one of helping nonspecialists understand the meaning of the results. Researchers conducting RCTs usually deal with the inability to study the effects of net recipients in part by confining their sample to people who are very likely to be net recipients—sometimes people toward the bottom of the net recipient range. They will report results for average comparisons between the control and experimental groups drawn from that subset of the population, but citizens and policymakers will be most interested in how the UBI affects the average person nationwide. If they interpret the numbers they read as being representative of the whole of the population, their understanding will highly exaggerate UBI's effects for good or bad—even if the study was an unbiased estimate of the segment of the population it sampled.

The following chapter considers how problems discussed so far affected the 1970s experiments.

CHAPTER 6

BIG Experiments of the 1970s and the Public Reaction to Them

Abstract This chapter discusses the five Negative Income Tax experiments conducted in the 1970s in the United States and Canada, summarizes their findings, and shows how badly they were misunderstood at the time. It argues that although the experiments succeeded in the scientific goal of obtaining useful data, they badly failed in the goal of improving public understanding of the issue. This experience provides extremely important lessons for the current round of basic income experiments.

Keywords SIME/DIME • Income maintenance experiments • Mincome • Basic income experiments • Negative Income Tax experiments • Social science experiments • Basic income • Universal Basic Income • Inequality • Poverty

Between 1968 and 1980, the US and Canadian governments conducted five NIT experiments. They got started when what I've called the second wave of the UBI movement was at its height. The United States had declared "War On Poverty." Civil rights activists were turning their attention to poverty and inequality. The United States was rethinking its welfare system with an eye to expanding and improving it. All of this created a strong interest in BIG, especially in the form of the NIT, but UBI (under various names) was also in the public discussion in the era. The last of

K. Widerquist, *A Critical Analysis of Basic Income Experiments for Researchers, Policymakers, and Citizens*, Exploring the Basic Income Guarantee, https://doi.org/10.1007/978-3-030-03849-6_6

these experiments wound down and their results came out at a time when expanding and improving the welfare system was much less popular.[1] This political context probably had a significant effect on the experiments and the reception of their results. Lessons from these experiments affect the argument throughout this book.

1 Labor Market Effects of the NIT Experiments of the 1970s

Unfortunately, most of the attention of the 1970s experiments was directed not at the effects of the policy (how it affects the welfare of net beneficiaries), but to one potential side effect (how it affects the labor time of test subjects). And so that issue takes up most of the discussion here. This section draws heavily on an earlier work, entitled, "A Failure to Communicate: What (If Anything) Can We Learn from the Negative Income Tax Experiments."[2]

Table 6.1 summarizes the basic facts of the five NIT experiments. The first four columns show the name of the experiment, where it was conducted, the years it ran, and its sample size, usually showing how much it decreased due to dropouts. The specifications of each experiment varied considerably and so the last three columns summarize information about the makeup of the people being studied, the grant level, and the marginal tax rate.

The largest NIT experiment was the SIME/DIME. The main study was conducted from 1970 to 1976 for most participants, but a small subsample (discussed in Chap. 4) continued to receive the grant until 1980.

The Canadian government initiated the Manitoba Basic Annual Income Experiment (Mincome) in 1975 when the US experiments were winding down. It was the only experiment to include a saturation study (along with an RCT). At the time of writing, Mincome remains the only BIG saturation study conducted in a higher-income nation. Disappointingly, by the time data collection was completed in 1978, interest in the guaranteed income was seriously on the wane and the Canadian government cancelled the project in 1980 before the data was fully analyzed. It would be decades before researchers would go back to it.

Scholarly and popular media articles on the NIT experiments focused, more than anything else, on the NIT's "work-" or "labor-effort response"—the comparison of how much the experimental group worked relative to the control group. Table 6.2 summarizes the findings of several

[1] Widerquist, "Three Waves of Basic Income Support."

[2] "A Failure to Communicate: What (If Anything) Can We Learn from the Negative Income Tax Experiments?"

Table 6.1 Summary of the Negative Income Tax experiments in the United States and Canada

Name	*Location(s)*	*Data collection*	*Sample size: initial (final)*	*Sample characteristics*	*Grant level*[a]	*Marginal tax rate*[b]
The New Jersey Graduated Work Incentive Experiment (NJ)	New Jersey and Pennsylvania	1968–1972	1216 (983)	Black, white, and Latino, two-parent families in urban areas with a male head aged 18–58 and income below 150% of the poverty line	0.5 0.75 1.00 1.25	0.3 0.5 0.7
The Rural Income-Maintenance Experiment (RIME)	Iowa and North Carolina	1970–1972	809 (729)	Both two-parent families and female-headed households in rural areas with income below 150% of poverty line	0.5 0.75 1.00	0.3 0.5 0.7
The Seattle/Denver Income Maintenance Experiments (SIME/DIME)	Seattle and Denver	1970–1976, (some to 1980)	4800	Black, white, and Latino families with at least one dependent and incomes below $11,000 for single parents, $13,000 for two-parent families	0.75, 1.26, 1.48	0.5 0.7, 0.7–0.025y, 0.8–0.025y[c]
The Gary, Indiana Experiment (Gary)	Gary, Indiana	1971–1974	1799 (967)	Black households, primarily female-headed, head 18–58, income below 240% of poverty line	0.75 1.0	0.4 0.6
The Manitoba Basic Annual Income Experiment (Mincome)	Winnipeg and Dauphin, Manitoba	1975–1978	1300	Families with, head younger than 58 and income below $13,000 for a family of four	C$3800 C$4800 C$5800	0.35 0.5 0.75

[a]The "grant level" or "guarantee level" is the maximum NIT level for a person or family with no income other than the NIT. This is the equivalent of the UBI level. US grant levels were reported as a percentage of the poverty line. Canadian grant levels were reported in Canadian dollars (C$)

[b]The "marginal tax rate" or the "take-back rate" is the rate at which the NIT is reduced as income rises. This is equivalent to the rate at which income is taxed in an income-tax-financed equivalent UBI

[c]"y" stands for family income

Source: Reproduced from Widerquist (2005)

Table 6.2 Summary of findings of labor-reduction effect

Study	*Data source*	*Labor reduction*[a] *(in hours per year*[b] *and percentage)*			*Comments and caveats*
		Husbands	*Wives*	*SFH*	
Robins (1985)	4 US[c]	−89 −5%	−117 −21.1%	−123 −13.2%	Study of studies that does not assess the methodology of the studies but simply combines their estimates; finds large consistency throughout, and "in no case is there evidence of a massive withdrawal from the labor force"; no assessment of whether the work response is large or small or its effect on cost; estimates apply to a poverty-line guarantee rate with a marginal tax rate of 50%
Burtless (1986)	4 US	−119 −7%	−93 −17%	−79 −7%	Average of results of the four US experiments weighted by sample size, except for the SFH estimates, which are a weighted average of the SIME/DIME and Gary results only
Keeley (1981)	4 US	−7.9%			A simple average of the estimates of 16 studies of the four US experiments
Robins and West (1980)	SIME/ DIME	−128.9 −7%	−165.9 −25%	−147.1 −15%	Estimates "labor supply effects"; it goes without saying that this is different from "labor-market effects"
Robins and West (1980)	SIME/ DIME	−9%	−20%	−25%	Recipients take 2.4 years to fully adjust their behavior to the new program
Cain et al. (1974)	NJ	–	−50 −20%	–	Includes caveats about the limited duration of the test and the representativeness of the sample; notes that the evidence shows a smaller effect than nonexperimental studies
Watts et al. (1974)	NJ	−1.4% to −6.6%	–	–	Depending on size of G and t

Rees and Watts (1976)	NJ	−1.5 hpw[b] −0.5%	−0.61%	–	Found anomalous positive effect on hours and earnings of blacks
Ashenfelter (1978)	RIME	−8%	−27%	–	"There must be serious doubt about the implications of the experimental results for the adoption of any permanent negative income tax program"
Moffitt (1979)	Gary	−3% to −6%	0%	−26% to −30%	No caveat about missing demand, but careful not to imply the results mean more than they do
Hum and Simpson (1993)	Mincome	−17 −1%	−15 −3%	−133 −17%	Smaller response to the Canadian experiment was not surprising because of the make-up of the sample and the treatments offered

[a]The negative signs indicate that the change in labor effort is a reduction
[b]Hours per year except where indicated "hpw," hours per week
[c]US refers to four US studies of the era; it excludes Canada and the studies conducted in the twenty-first century

NJ New Jersey graduated work incentive experiment; *SIME/DIME* Seattle/Denver income maintenance experiment; *Gary* Gary income maintenance experiment; *RIME* rural income maintenance experiment; *Mincome* Manitoba income maintenance experiment; *SFH* single female "head of household"

Source: Reproduced from Widerquist (2005)

of the studies on the labor-effort response to the NIT experiments, showing the difference in hours (the "labor reduction") by the experimental group relative to the control group in foregone hours per year and in percentage terms. Results are reported for three categories of laborers, husbands, wives, and "single female heads" (SFH), which meant single mothers. The relative labor reduction varied substantially across the five experiments from 0.5% to 9.0% for husbands, which means that the experimental group worked less than the control group by about 0.5 hour to 4 hours per week, 20–130 hours per year, or 1–4 fulltime weeks per year. Three studies averaged the results from the four US experiments and found relative labor-reduction effects in the range of 5–7.9%.[3] One study using computer simulations estimated that the labor reduction in response to a national program would be only about one-third of the reduction in the Gary experiment (1.6% rather than 4.5%) because the sample was drawn from a relatively small portion of the population (people living near or below the poverty line).[4]

The response of wives and single mothers was somewhat larger in terms of hours and substantially larger in percentage terms because they tended to work fewer hours, to begin with. Wives reduced their labor effort by 0–27% and single mothers reduced their labor effort by 15–30%. These percentages correspond to reductions of about 0–166 hours per year. The labor-market response of wives had a much larger range than the other two groups, but this was usually attributed to the peculiarities of the labor markets in Gary and Winnipeg, where particularly small responses were found.

Studies that I reviewed did not place great stress on how reliable estimates were considered to be of the possible national response. Most of the data I have below represents point estimates of the difference between the control and experimental groups rather than confidence intervals or estimates of the national response.

[3] G. Burtless, "The Work Response to a Guaranteed Income. A Survey of Experimental Evidence," in *Lessons from the Income Maintenance Experiments*, ed. A. H. Munnell (Boston: Federal Reserve Bank of Boston, 1986). M.C. Keeley, *Labor Supply and Public Policy: A Critical Review* (New York: Academic Press, 1981). P.K. Robins, "A Comparison of the Labor Supply Findings from the Four Negative Income Tax Experiments," *Journal of Human Resources* 20, no. 4 (1985).

[4] R.A. Moffitt, "The Labor Supply Response in the Gary Experiment," ibid. 14 (1979).

All or most of the figures reported above are raw comparisons between the control and experimental groups: they are not predictions of how labor-market participation is likely to change in response to a national NIT or UBI. Consider four of the many reasons why.

First, participants tended to be drawn from a small segment of the population: people with incomes near the poverty line. This part of the income distribution is about where one would expect the largest negative labor-effort effect because the potential grant is high relative to their earned income. Thus, the response of the group studied is likely to be much larger than the response of the entire labor force to a national program. As mentioned above, one study using computer simulations estimated that the labor reduction in the Gary experiment (4.5%) would translate into a 1.6% labor-effort reduction in a national program.[5] I wonder whether numbers like 1.6%—more easily perceived as negligible—would have had a different effect on the discussion of the results at the time.

Second, the figures do not include any demand response, which economic theory predicts would lead to higher wages and a partial reversal of the labor reduction (see this chapter). One study using simulation techniques to estimate the demand response found it to be small.[6] Another found that, "[r]eduction in labor supply produced by these programs does tend to raise low-skill wages, and this improves transfer efficiency."[7] That is, it increases the benefit to recipients from each dollar of public spending.

Third, the figures were reported in average hours per week and very often misinterpreted to imply that 5–7.9% of primary breadwinners dropped out of the labor force. In fact, few, if any workers simply dropped out of the labor force for the duration of the study, as knee-jerk reactions to guaranteed income proposals often assume.[8] Primary breadwinners in both the experiment and control groups left their jobs (whether voluntarily or by getting fired or laid off) at about the same rate. The observed

[5] Ibid.

[6] D.H. Greenberg, "Some Labor Market Effects of Labor Supply Responses to Transfer Programs," *Social-Economic Planning Sciences* 17, no. 4 (1983).

[7] J.H. Bishop, "The General Equilibrium Impact of Alternative Antipoverty Strategies," *Industrial and Labor Relations Review* 32, no. 2 (1979).

[8] Robert Levine et al., "A Retrospective on the Negative Income Tax Experiments: Looking Back at the Most Innovative Field Studies in Social Policy," in *The Ethics and Economics of the Basic Income Guarantee*, ed. Karl Widerquist, Michael A. Lewis, and Steven Pressman (Aldershot: Ashgate, 2005).

labor-effort reduction was mainly caused by workers in the experimental group taking longer to find their next job if and when they became nonemployed.

Fourth, the experimental group's labor "reduction" was only a relative reduction in comparison to the control group. Although this language is standard for experimental studies, it is often wrongly taken to imply that receiving the NIT was the major determinant of labor hours. In fact, in some studies, labor hours increased for both groups, and in all studies, the labor hours of both groups tended to rise and fall together along with the macroeconomic health of the economy—implying that when good jobs were plentiful, both groups took them, but when they were less plentiful, the control group searched harder or accepted less attractive jobs.[9]

A bigger problem than misinterpretations of the size of the labor-effort reduction was that most laypeople writing about the NIT experiments assumed any labor reduction, no matter how small, was an extremely negative side effect. But it is not obviously desirable to put unemployed workers in the position where they are desperate to start their next job as soon as possible. It's obviously bad for workers and families to be in that position. It's not only difficult to go through, but also it reduces their ability to command desirable wages and working conditions. Increased periods of nonemployment might have a social benefit if they lead to better matches between workers and firms.

Another problem with the focus on labor effort was that it distracted attention from the question of how well the NIT achieved its main goals of reducing poverty and increasing the well-being of low-income people. Assessing these issues requires looking at nonlabor-market effects.

2 Nonlabor-Market Effects of the NIT Experiments

The experimental results for various quality-of-life indicators were substantial and encouraging. Some studies found significant positive influences in elementary school attendance rates, teacher ratings, and test scores. Some studies found that children in the experimental group stayed in school significantly longer than children in the control group. Some found an increase in adults going on to continuing education. Some of the experiments found

[9] Widerquist, "A Failure to Communicate: What (If Anything) Can We Learn from the Negative Income Tax Experiments?"

desirable effects on many important quality-of-life indicators, including reduced incidents of low-birth-weight babies, decreased household indebtedness, increased food consumption, improvements in medical treatment, and increased nutritional content of the diet, especially among children. Some even found reduced domestic abuse and reduced psychiatric emergencies.[10]

Much of the attention to nonlabor-market effects focused not on the presumed goals of the policy but on another side effect: a controversial finding that the experimental group in SIME/DIME had a higher divorce rate than the control group. Researchers argued forcefully on both sides into the early 1990s, with no conclusive resolution in the literature. The finding was not replicated by the Manitoba experiment, which found a lower divorce rate in the experimental group. The higher divorce rate in some studies examining SIME/DIME was widely presented as a negative effect, even though the only explanation researchers had for it was that the NIT must have relieved women from financial dependence on husbands.[11] It is at the very least questionable to label one spouse staying with another solely because of financial dependence as a "good" thing.

3 An Overall Assessment?

Most of the researchers involved considered the results extremely promising overall. Comparisons of the control and experimental groups indicated that the NIT was capable of significantly reducing the material effects of poverty, and the relative reductions in labor effort were probably within the affordable range and almost certainly within the sustainable range.

But experiments of this type were not capable of producing a bottom line. Nonspecialists examining the results were left asking: what *was* the cost exactly? How much were the material effects of poverty reduced? What is the verdict from an overall comparison of costs and benefits?

As this book argues throughout, experiments cannot answer these questions, although they can contribute towards attempts to address these questions. Simply reporting experimental comparison without explaining what they contribute to these larger issues leads to misunderstanding—as the following section illustrates.

[10] Levine et al.

[11] Ibid.; Widerquist, "A Failure to Communicate: What (If Anything) Can We Learn from the Negative Income Tax Experiments?"

4 Public Reaction to the Release of NIT Experimental Findings in the 1970s

As promising as the results were to the researchers involved, the NIT experiments were seriously misunderstood in the public discussion at the time. The discussion in Congress and in the popular media displayed little understanding of the complexity of experimental results or difficulties of extrapolating them into answers to any bottom-line question. The results were spun or misunderstood and used in simplistic arguments to reject any form of guaranteed income offhand.

The experiments were of most interest to Congress during the period from 1970 to 1972, when President Nixon's Family Assistance Plan (FAP), which had elements of an NIT, was under debate in Congress. None of the experiments were ready to release final reports at the time. Congress insisted researchers produce some kind of preliminary report, which was criticized by members of Congress for being "premature," just as researchers had warned.[12]

Results of the fourth and largest experiment, SIME/DIME, were released while Congress was debating a policy proposed by President Carter, which had already moved quite away from the NIT model. Dozens of technical reports with large amounts of data were simplified down to two statements: NIT decreased labor effort and supposedly increased divorce. The smallness of the labor disincentive effect hardly drew any attention. Although from the start, researchers expected some labor-reduction effect and were pleased to find it was small enough to make the program affordable, many members of Congress and popular media commentators acted as if the mere existence of a labor-reduction effect was enough to disqualify the program.

The public discussion displayed little, if any, understanding that the 5–7.9% difference between the control and experimental groups is not a prediction of the national response. In an earlier work, I reviewed nonacademic articles on the experiments and found that they had little or no understanding that the labor-effort response would be much smaller as a percentage of the entire population, that it could potentially be counteracted by the availability of good jobs, or that it could be the first step necessary for workers to command higher wages and better working conditions, which could partly counteract the labor-reduction effect.[13]

[12] "A Failure to Communicate: What (If Anything) Can We Learn from the Negative Income Tax Experiments?"

[13] Ibid.

The United Press International simply got the facts wrong, saying the SIME/DIME study showed, "adults might abandon efforts to find work," as did *the Rocky Mountain News*, which claimed that the NIT "saps the recipients' desire to work." The *Seattle Times* presented a relatively well-rounded understanding of the results, but despite this, it simply concluded that the existence of any decline in labor effort—regardless of size—was enough to "cast doubt" on the plan.

Others went even farther, saying that the existence of a work-disincentive effect was enough to declare the experiments a failure. Headlines such as "Income Plan Linked to Less Work" and "Guaranteed Income Against Work Ethic" appeared in newspapers following the hearings. Only a few exceptions such as Carl Rowan for the *Washington Star* considered that it might be acceptable for people working in bad jobs to work less, but he could not figure out why the government would spend so much money to find out whether people work less when you pay them to stay home.[14]

Senator Daniel Patrick Moynihan, who was one of the few social scientists in the Senate, also failed to understand the experimental findings. He wrote, "But were we wrong about a guaranteed income! Seemingly it is calamitous. It increases family dissolution ..., decreases work, etc. Such is now the state of the science, and it seems to me we are honor bound to abide by it for the moment." Senator Bill Armstrong, mentioning *only the existence* of a labor-disincentive effect, declared the NIT "An acknowledged failure," writing, "Let's admit it, learn from it, and move on."[15]

Robert Spiegelman, one of the directors of SIME/DIME, defended the experiments in an op-ed piece, in which he argued that the experiments provided much-needed cost estimates that demonstrated the feasibility of the NIT. He said that the decline in labor effort was not dramatic and could not understand why so many commentators drew such different conclusions than the experimenters. Gary Burtless remarked, "Policymakers and policy analysts ... seem far more impressed by our certainty that the efficiency price of redistribution is positive than they are by the equally persuasive evidence that the price is small."[16]

The experiments produced a great deal of useful evidence, but failed to communicate those results either to Congress or to the public. The literature review reveals neither supporters nor opponents who appeared to

[14] Ibid.
[15] Ibid.
[16] Burtless.

have a better understanding of the likely effects of the NIT or any income guarantee in the discussions following the release of the results of the experiments in the 1970s.[17]

The late-1970s reaction to experimental results reflected the times, as politicians like Ronald Reagan were attracting support to the idea of cutting the welfare system rather than expanding and improving it, often by vilifying almost anyone who was eligible for redistributive programs. Many of the commentaries on the SIME/DIME results reflected such a perspective, but I would caution against reading too much into the timing. The complaint about giving too much support to the sturdy beggar has been a perennial demagogic talking point in English-speaking countries since the Elizabethan era. And it remains a tempting talking point for opponents of redistribution almost anywhere. Thus, while keeping the context in mind, I ask readers to consider the potential that this experience might contain more widely applicable lessons.

Whatever the causes of it, an environment with a low understanding of complexity is highly vulnerable to spin with simplistic or even vacuous interpretation. All sides spin, but in the late-1970s NIT debate, only one side showed up. The guaranteed income movement that had been so active in the United States at the beginning of the decade had declined to the point that it was able to provide little or no counterspin to the enormously negative discussion of the experimental results in the popular media.

Whether the low-information content of the discussion in the media resulted more from spin, sensationalism, or honest misunderstanding is hard to determine. But whatever the reasons, the low-information discussion of the experimental results put the NIT (and, in hindsight, UBI by proxy) in an extremely unfavorable light, when the scientific results were mixed to favorable.

Researchers working on the experiments were blind-sided by the level of spin. They had not been asked to make special efforts to explain their results to laypeople in a way that would head off possible spin. If they had been asked, they would have had no particular expertise in doing so. And even if they or some science communication specialist had tried, it would have been extremely difficult, if not impossible, to communicate the complexities to most nonspecialists in the time a reasonable person typically devotes to the issue.

[17] Widerquist, "A Failure to Communicate: What (If Anything) Can We Learn from the Negative Income Tax Experiments?"

Thus, it would be wrong simply to blame researchers for failing to communicate their results clearly. The problem came from the inherent difficulty of communicating complex and tentative scientific findings to a lay audience looking for definitive answers on questions that are only partly related to those findings. Everyone involved has a responsibility not to be blind-sided by spin and misunderstanding next time. The political context will be different, but the warning needs to be considered. The rest of this book is an effort to help reduce similar misunderstandings in future experiments.

CHAPTER 7

New Experimental Findings 2008–2013

Abstract This chapter discusses findings from two recent Universal Basic Income (UBI) experiments conducted in the late 2000s and early 2010s and from earlier experimental data that was released in the same period. This chapter shows how these findings had a more positive impact on public understanding of UBI and related policies than the release of data from the 1970s NIT experiments.

Keywords Basic income experiments • Negative Income Tax experiments • Social science experiments • Basic income • Universal Basic Income • Inequality • Poverty

Experimental results continued to trickle out and were debated in academic journals in the early 1990s. No new experimental findings came out until the late 2000s when interest in BIG experiments gradually resumed.

Canada's Mincome experiment was cancelled before most of its findings were assessed. As many as 1800 boxes of file folders were left unexamined until 2009, when a researcher named Evelyn Forget got a grant to begin reexamining them. Perhaps she did a better job of explaining the findings in a way that people understood, or perhaps the political situation at the time made for a more receptive audience. But whatever the reason, the newly released Mincome findings had a much more positive impact on the UBI

K. Widerquist, *A Critical Analysis of Basic Income Experiments for Researchers, Policymakers, and Citizens*, Exploring the Basic Income Guarantee, https://doi.org/10.1007/978-3-030-03849-6_7

debate than the NIT experimental findings released in the 1970s. Forget dubbed Mincome's saturation site (Dauphin, Manitoba) "the Town with No Poverty" and the media picked up on it. Media reports stressed the effects (rather than the side effects) of Mincome. These effects included reductions in hospitalizations, especially for mental health and accidents. Forget estimated the national savings that would occur if the decline in hospital visits was replicated nationally.[1] Media reports discussing the labor-market impact did so in context, even discussing how the lack of pressure to find another job helped people land the right job. Whether labor-market findings were better received because of how they were reported or because of the tenor of the times is difficult to determine, but undoubtedly Forget, drawing on previous experience, was more aware of the need to put those findings in a context that laypeople could understand.

The first UBI experiments of the twenty-first century were conducted in Namibia (2008–2009) and India (2011–2013). They differed from the 1970s experiments in at least four important ways. First, they focused on UBI rather than NIT, reflecting the change in the discussion of BIG over the intervening 30 years. Second, they were funded primarily by private institutions rather than the government. Third, both of them took place at a time when BIG was not a major part of the political discussion in the countries where they were conducted. Fourth, they took place in very different political contexts, most strikingly that they took place in less wealthy countries with much deeper poverty. Different issues took primary importance. Poverty, education, and empowering women were the most important to researchers than work incentives and/or interactions with the existing welfare system.

The Namibian study found extremely promising results, including significant decreases in household poverty, child malnutrition, underweight children, household debt, crime, and so on. Results also included significant increases in economic activity, access to medication and healthcare, school attendance, and household savings. Predicted effects of increased alcohol consumption did not come true: people receiving the UBI drank the same as typical Namibians. This issue of whether people would spend the UBI on alcohol took on a prominent role in the UBI discussion in Namibia, much like the labor-effort response in the US and Canadian

[1] Evelyn L. Forget, "The Town with No Poverty: The Health Effects of a Canadian Guaranteed Annual Income Field Experiment," *Canadian Public Policy* 37, no. 3 (2011).

contexts. Probably the most striking difference between the Namibia project and the NIT experiments was that the labor-effort response was positive. That is, people receiving UBI worked more.[2] The expected explanation was that the depth of poverty and the level of unemployment in Namibia make it hard for people to work as much as they might want to. With more of their basic needs met and more economic activity in the area, people were able to work more.

The Indian project found similar promising results. Results included significant decreases in illness, child labor, household indebtedness, and so one. Women were found transitioning into different occupations. Some women who were already committed to a primary occupation added a second. Recipients also invested more in self-employment activities. Results also included significant improvements in food consumption, medical treatment, school attendance, school performance, household savings, and so on. Like the Namibian study, the Indian study found that people receiving UBI worked more than people in the control group and drank at the same rate as people in the control group.[3]

The twenty-first-century reports from Mincome and the reports from India and Namibia were well reported and better understood in the press. All three sets of findings were reported at a time when UBI was far out of the political maintain stream and was receiving very little media attention in these countries and around most of the world. All three brought significant international media attention to UBI, which may have contributed to the gradual increase in support for the UBI movement that has gone on ever since.[4]

[2] Claudia Haarmann et al., *Making the Difference: The Big in Namibia: Basic Income Grant Pilot Project Assessment Report* (Windhoek: Basic Income Grant Coalition, 2009).

[3] Guy Standing, "Unconditional Basic Income: Two Pilots in Madhya Pradesh," in *Conference on Unconditional Cash Transfers: Findings of two pilot studies* (New Delhi: Sewa, 2013).

[4] Widerquist, "Three Waves of Basic Income Support."

CHAPTER 8

Current, Planned, and Proposed Experiments, 2014–Present

Abstract This chapter briefly discusses some of the now ongoing Universal Basic Income (UBI) experiments, proposed UBI experiments, and experiments in policies similar to UBI. The book references these experiments only rarely, because its goal is not to analyze or criticize them, but to offer some useful analysis to the people commissioning, designing, conducting, reporting on, and reading about them.

Keywords Basic income experiments • Negative Income Tax experiments • Social science experiments • Basic income • GiveDirectly • Universal Basic Income • Inequality • Poverty

This chapter gives a brief overview of the UBI trials that are underway, planned, or at least under discussion around the world right now. But it will be brief for three reasons.

First, the role of this book is not to criticize these experiments; it merely offers (hopefully useful) analysis about how to conduct and discuss the results of UBI experiments across a broad range of contexts. Therefore, specifics of any particular experiment are not directly relevant to my analysis unless that experiment happens to provide a useful example.

Second, the planning process of UBI experiments is extremely fluid. Anything I write now will be out-of-date quickly. It is impossible to come

K. Widerquist, *A Critical Analysis of Basic Income Experiments for Researchers, Policymakers, and Citizens*, Exploring the Basic Income Guarantee, https://doi.org/10.1007/978-3-030-03849-6_8

up with a definitive list of existing and planned UBI experiments because it is uncertain whether some planned or discussed experiments will actually take place or whether they will deviate from the UBI model as they get beyond the planning stages.

Third, it is difficult to determine whether something qualifies as a UBI experiment, both because of the difficulty of deciding whether the proposal under scrutiny is universal and unconditional enough to qualify as a "UBI" and because of the difficulty of defining "experiment," as discussed above.

That said, here's the overview.

Like the 1970s experiments, the current round of experiments appears at a time when concern about poverty and inequality is rising, people are rethinking the existing redistributive strategy, and BIG is an issue in mainstream politics. The context is otherwise very different. The welfare state has been under attack and greatly pared back in many countries since the 1970s, where it had been gradually expanding for decades. The concern that automation disrupts the labor force, which played a small but significant part in the 1960s and 1970s BIG movement, now plays a far larger role in the debate today. The two US experiments are both largely funded by tech entrepreneurs who are particularly concerned about this issue. One might think that the increased concern with automation would decrease the concern that UBI might decease labor effort, but this does not seem to be the case in most places. Many still seem to tacitly assume that decreased labor effort is necessarily a bad thing.

The current round of experiments is taking place all over the world, rather than just in Anglo-America. Including the Namibian and Indian projects discussed in the last chapter, the current round involves experiments on four different continents, in high-, middle-, and low-income countries and in countries with strong or weak welfare systems. The different contexts make different testing opportunities possible, but they also bring in new constraints because researchers have to comply with local laws, which can significantly constrain the project. This is particularly important in Europe, where experiments have to comply with national and European Union law.

Researchers in different political contexts are understandably interested in very different questions, but considering each experiment as a part of an international effort is useful for at least three reasons. First, researchers might consider attempting to replicate each other's findings with different methods and/or in different circumstances. Second, researchers might try to look for things that other experiments have neglected to examine. Third, researchers might learn how to defend their experiments from criticism that they had not expected in their political context.

Researchers today obviously have access to more sophisticated computer statistics programs, but the logistical and financial difficulties of distributing cash to hundreds or thousands of people remain. Therefore, the experiments today are, for the most part, comparable in size and scope to the 1970s experiments. Only in less wealthy countries have significantly larger experiments become feasible.

The next several sections give a brief review of several current or proposed experiments on or closely relating to UBI.

1 GiveDirectly in Kenya

The US-based nonprofit organization GiveDirectly is conducting the world's largest UBI experiment in Kenya. The project is motivated largely by the desire for an evidence-based approach to international aid, and the belief that evidence so far indicates that the poorest people in the world benefit more from cash than from other forms of aid. The experiment will involve tens of thousands of people across about 200 treatment and 100 control villages for several years. It will combine the techniques of RCTs and saturation studies with a significant number of control and experimental villages. The project is able to be so large both because GiveDirectly has raised a lot of money and because Kenya has such deep poverty. Most villages will receive US$0.75 dollars per day, in monthly payments—some for 2 years, some for 12 years. A few villages will receive one lump-sum payment of $500.

The low level of the UBI in the GiveDirectly project is necessary because of the great poverty and inequality in Kenya. Many of the villages where GiveDirectly operates have average incomes less than $1 per day. If GiveDirectly were to give everyone in one village $2 per day, they might make that village four-times-richer than the control or nonparticipating village down the road. This could create animosity and resistance to the program. Until GiveDirectly can afford to give the grant to everyone in Kenya, it has to be small.

The small size of the grant makes a very large study possible. Researchers for GiveDirectly are able to combine RCT and saturation techniques and to run a fairly long-term study that is likely to produce a great deal of valuable data about how UBI affects various quality-of-life indicators. Although the effects of a very small UBI on severely impoverished villages in Kenya might not tell us a lot about how a large UBI will work in wealthier nations, this study promises to provide a great deal of useful information about how UBI will work in less wealthy nations—where it is needed the most.[1]

2 Finland

As I write, Finland is nearing completion of a small-scale, 2-year UBI experiment, which is being conducted by Kela, the Finnish Social Insurance Institution. It involves about 2000 participants between ages 25 and 58, selected by a nationwide random sample of people receiving unemployment benefits. The experiment replaces unemployment insurance benefits of €560 per month with a UBI of the same size. The Finnish parliament rewrote the law to make participation in the experiment mandatory for unemployment benefit recipients who were selected.

The Finnish effort has been criticized because the UBI is so low and because, being drawn from people receiving unemployment benefits, it incorporates the conditions of eligibility attached to those unemployment benefits. Kela responded that it simply does not have the budget to conduct an experiment across a large selection of low-income individuals.[2]

The makeup of the Finish experiment has at least two advantages as a UBI test. First, the small grant makes it comparable to the existing program, eliminating problems of distinguishing the effects of the size and type of program under investigation (as discussed in Chap. 4). Second, even though people had to be eligible for unemployment benefits to be selected for the study, once they were assigned to the experimental group, conditionality was eliminated. Therefore, although the study is not designed to examine how a large UBI would affect a large cross section of the public, it is well designed to examine how a small UBI would affect people currently on unemployment benefits. And that kind of study can reveal a great deal of useful information.

The stated goal of the Finnish experiment is "[t]o obtain information on the effects of a basic income on employment."[3] This concern is very similar

[1] https://givedirectly.org/

[2] Olli Kangas, "Final Report for the Finnish Basic Income Experiment Recommends That the Experiment Be Expanded," (Helsinki, Finland: Kela, 2017); "From Idea to Experiment: Report on Universal Basic Income Experiment in Finland," in *Working Papers* (Helsinki, Finland: Kela, 2016).

[3] Olli Kangas, Miska Simanainen, and Pertti Honkanen, "Basic Income in the Finnish Context," *Intereconomics* 52, no. 2 (2017).

to what became the focus of the four US experiments in the 1970s, but the design and focus of the study makes it very different. One of the motivations of the experiment is the fear that Finland's long-term unemployment insurance eligibility criteria created a poverty trap. Because the Finnish project tests UBI only on people currently receiving unemployment benefits (i.e. people currently not working) and because UBI eliminates eligibility criteria that might inhibit unemployed people from taking jobs, the study might find that UBI *increases* employment among study participants. The study does not increase marginal tax rates for participants and so it will provide a much higher overall income for people in the study,[4] but it will be expensive to replicate that program design on a national scale.

3 Canada

The Ontario government briefly conducted a UBI-related experiment at three sites in Ontario: Hamilton, Thunder Bay, and Lindsay, with hopes of later including an additional study at a First Nations community, but the entire study was abruptly cancelled when the provincial government changed.

The experiment, which was inspired by issues such as poverty, inequality, and the complexity of the social insurance system, involved an experimental group of up to 4000 low-income people aged 18–64. Researchers hoped to examine the effects of a UBI-like policy on quality-of-life indicators as well as on work behavior, education, and entrepreneurship.[5] It remains to be seen whether the project lasted long enough to get useful data.

Although the people conducting the study call it a "basic income," it is a negative income tax—conditional not only on household income, but also on household size. Single people receive a maximum of C$16,989 per year, while couples receive a maximum of C$24,027.[6] This added condition is not necessary for the purpose of approximating UBI with an NIT in an experiment. The motivation for it is probably to save money. Two people living together can live more cheaply than two people living apart. By including this condition, the program can provide a poverty-level BIG at a lower cost, but it might create incentive problems.

[4] Ibid.

[5] Ministry of Community and Social Services, "Ontario's Basic Income Pilot: Studying the Impact of a Basic Income," ed. Ontario Ministry of Community and Social Services (Toronto: Queen's Printer for Ontario, 2018); E. L. Forget et al., "Pilot Lessons: How to Design a Basic Income Pilot Project for Ontario," in *Mowat Research* (Toronto: Mowat Centre, 2016).

[6] Ministry of Community and Social Services; Forget et al.

4 Y Combinator in the United States

Y Combinator Research (YCR)—the nonprofit arm of Y Combinator—is a private venture capital firm in the United States. It is run by tech entrepreneurs motivated by the automation issue. Basic income has become a major focus of YCR's research, and the organization has taken on the effort to fund a large-scale UBI project with purely private funds.

Originally planned for Oakland, California, the organizers decided to move the experiment to two other states not yet announced. The experimental group will involve at least 1000 people who will receive $1000 per month for 3–5 years. More subjects will be included if funding allows. The experimental group will involve people aged 21–40 with total household incomes (in the year before enrollment) below the median income in their local community. Although researchers will gather data on how participants use their time and money, they will focus on the impact of UBI on social and physiological well-being—using both subjective and objective measures. The initial project proposal makes no mention of phasing out the grant as income rises.[7] Therefore, YCR is testing a true UBI, but like the Finnish study, the YCR study implicitly assumes that net beneficiaries will face no higher marginal tax rates under a national UBI system than they do now.

5 The Netherlands

The Dutch experiment is a bit unusual for the times. While politicians in Greece, Italy, Spain, and several other places are promoting proposals that are called "basic income," even though they share little with the basic income model, the Netherlands is experimenting with something that they do not call "basic income," even though it takes a significant step in the direction of it. The experiment seems to be motived in part by dissatisfaction with so-called active labor-market policies that are in place in the Netherlands and several other countries. These policies allow people to keep some benefits while in work, but subject them to harsh sanctions if they fail to search for work or to remain in work if they find it.[8]

[7] Y Combinator Research, "Basic Income Project Proposal" (Oakland, CA: Y Combinator Research, 2017).

[8] Loek Groot and Robert van der Veen, remarks made at the workshop on basic income experiments held at the Center for International and Regional Studies, Georgetown University in Qatar, March 26, 2018.

Although the Dutch experiment is limited to welfare recipients under the current system, it frees people from job requirements of the current system and allows them to keep some of their benefits as they earn. These are two important features of a UBI. Because the cost-effectiveness record of active labor-market policies is mixed, some researchers have hope that steps in the direction of UBI will prove to be a more cost-effective means of achieving some of the ends of active labor-market policies.[9]

The Dutch experiment is sometimes conceived of as a "trust" experiment because the existing system makes caseworkers responsible for enforcing rather draconian sanctions on recipients, fostering distrust on both sides. Yet, this experiment conceptualizes "trust" in terms of fulfilling the obligations of a recipient of conventional social assistance—primarily to take work if they find it. In that sense, they are not directly related to UBI, which is often conceived as a rejection of such obligations.

The Dutch experiment is actually several experiments that will take place in several different municipalities across the country—made possible by a 2015 law permitting municipal experimentation. The experiments, launched in late 2017 and expected to last for 2 years, will study the effects on labor market and social participation, and health and well-being of allowing social assistance claimants to maintain at least some of their benefits as their income rises while exempting them from the legal duties of seeking work and/or participating in training activities. The experiments involve several different experimental groups eligible for slightly different policies. Recipients are randomly assigned to the control group or one of the experimental groups in their municipality.[10]

[9] Jochen Kluve, "The Effectiveness of European Active Labour Market Programs," *Labour Economics* 17, no. 6 (2010); S. Bouquin, "Social Minima in Europe: The Risks of Cumulating Income-Sources," in *The Ethics and Economics of the Basic Income Guarantee*, ed. Karl Widerquist, M. A. Lewis, and S. Pressman (Aldershot, UK: Ashgate, 2005). Loek Groot and Robert van der Veen, remarks made at the workshop on basic income experiments held at the Center for International and Regional Studies, Georgetown University in Qatar, March 26, 2018.

[10] Kate McFarland, "Overview of Current Basic Income Related Experiments," *Basic Income News*, October 19, 2017 2017; Loek F M Groot and Timo Verlaat, "The Rationale Behind the Utrecht Experiment," (2016).

6 Stockton, California

The city of Stockton, California, has secured funding from private nonprofits to launch a small-scale UBI project called "the Stockton Economic Empowerment Demonstration" (SEED). It will have about 100 participants receiving $500 a month for approximately 18 months. Like Y Combinator, major funders of the Stockton project are also largely involved in the tech industry and motivated by the automation issue.

Although SEED has received a great deal of media attention, it is in the early planning stages and few details have been announced. The organizers do not claim to be planning a "scientific experiment," but "a demonstration," which could be taken as an indication that it is aimed not to gather rigorous data but to further UBI politically.[11] There is nothing wrong with conducting a smaller-scale and/or a less rigorous study for political purposes as long as the results are presented honestly. Therefore, all the difficulties of clearly communicating what it does and does not say about the implementation of a full, nationwide UBI still apply.

7 Other Experiments

Barcelona is conducting an experiment it calls "B-Mincome" in honor of the earlier Canadian experiment. The project's literature draws inspiration from the UBI movement. The experiment involves about 1000 people grouped into ten small experimental groups and a control group of 1000 people. The various experimental groups will receive an NIT, some unconditionally and others attaching various conditional programs designed to encourage labor, entrepreneurship, community service, and so on.[12]

The Scottish government has committed funds to conduct a full-scale UBI experiment and is working with the Royal Society for the Encouragement of Arts, Manufactures and Commerce (RSA) and other institutions to design the project, but the experiment is currently in the planning stages. Few, if any, details about the experiment have been announced.[13]

[11] SEED, "A Guaranteed Income Demonstration," Stockton Economic Empowerment Demonstration, https://www.stocktondemonstration.org/

[12] Laura Colini, "The B-Mincome Project Journal N°1," (Barcelona: The City of Barcelona, 2017).

[13] McFarland.

The government of British Columbia, Canada, recently announced that it will conduct a UBI experiment, but it is only in the planning stages. Few details have been announced.[14]

There are many small UBI projects that aren't necessarily intended as experiments. Small-scale charities, such as "ReCivitas" in Brazil and "Eight" in Uganda, have been using the UBI model to help people for years.[15] A crowdfunding project in Germany, which has spilled over to the United States, has raised money to provide a basic income for a few randomly selected people.[16] A group of filmmakers have raised enough money to give a UBI of $231 per adult per week and $77 per child to about 20 people across eight states. The filmmakers will follow the recipients for 2 years, eventually producing a feature film or a television series, entitled "Bootstraps," to document how the grant affects their lives.[17] Because these projects are so small and because they are not primarily focused on data gathering, they seldom make the list of experiments.

Other experiments of varying size and connectedness to UBI are being discussed or at least rumored around the world, in places such as France, Korea, Iceland, Liberia, Manitoba, and Switzerland. Some of these initiatives might come to fruition, but I have little information about them.

8 Will We Refight the Last War?

When the current experiments start releasing their findings, the reaction will probably be very different than it was in the 1970s. Much of that discussion was particular to the place and time, which, as mentioned, was particularly unfavorable to UBI by the time most results were released. Nevertheless, it is almost certain that some problems of that era will reappear: lay audiences will have difficulty understanding the relevance of the results, and less conscientious supporters and opponents will attempt to seize on whatever findings they can to spin the discussion in their favor. More conscientious participants of the discussion—whether directly involved in the experiments or not—with the benefit of past experience, need to be ready this time.

[14] British-Columbia-Government, "Researchers Explore the Potential of Basic Income in B.C.," (Victoria: BC Gov News, 2018).

[15] Recivitas.org; Eight.world

[16] mein-grundeinkommen.de

[17] Bootstrapsfilm.com

I doubt the divorce issue will come back, but because the vilification of any nonwealthy person who balks at long hours for low pay is such a perennial favorite of the opponents of virtually any redistributive measure, people need to be ready for this sort of framing of the labor-effort issue, even if they do not expect it in their political context.

Labor effort was not a major issue in India or Namibia because in those areas, UBI was associated with increased work time. Similar results are expected in Kenya. The Finnish and Dutch experiments draw their samples in a way that is less likely to show a negative correlation between UBI and labor effort and may even show a positive correlation because of the focus on people already receiving benefits and relieving conditions associated with a poverty trap.

The other experiments are more likely to show negative correlations between UBI and labor effort. It is not certain that future experiments will find that negative correlation: the economy has changed a great deal in the last 40 or 50 years. But experimenters should be ready because if the UBI is substantial, the labor-effort response is very likely to be negative.[18] People involved should consider ways to preempt or counteract any spin based on such correlation in case they find it.

Of course, there are many other issues that people might use to spin the results of new UBI experiments. The issues will vary significantly by time and place. Knowing the role of experiments in the political economy of UBI, both internationally and in specific political context will help people preempt and/or counteract spin.

[18] Van Parijs and Vanderborght, p. 145.

CHAPTER 9

The Political Economy of the Decision to Have a UBI Experiment

Abstract This chapter discusses the surprisingly complex political economy of the decision process that brings about Universal Basic Income (UBI) experiments in response to a movement more interested in the immediate introduction of UBI than in experimentation with it. It shows that the process by which UBI experiments tend to come about makes them especially vulnerable to misunderstanding, sensationalism, and spin, which in turn make experiments a risky strategy for the UBI movement.

Keywords Basic income experiments • Negative Income Tax experiments • Social science experiments • Basic income • Universal Basic Income • Inequality • Poverty

The effort to understand the role of experiments in the political economy of the UBI discussion begins with an understanding of the strategic decision to have a UBI experiment.

There are many scientific reasons for a UBI trial. Such a trial can shed light on at least some of the controversial questions about UBI's practical effects, but scientific curiosity is not why trials are happening. They are an outcome of the political process.

UBI experiments are too large to be funded by a routine research grant. They are not the kind of project that can be initiated by a professor filling

K. Widerquist, *A Critical Analysis of Basic Income Experiments for Researchers, Policymakers, and Citizens*, Exploring the Basic Income Guarantee, https://doi.org/10.1007/978-3-030-03849-6_9

out a grant proposal. They are such major undertakings that all five of the 1970s experiments and four of the twenty-first-century experiments were created by acts of national or regional legislatures. The other five trials (Kenya, India, Namibia, Y Combinator, and Stockton, California) were all initiated by people closely connected to the UBI movement, who gathered support from well-funded people and institutions. That is, they too are an outcome of the political process.

Therefore, the demand for trials is a response to the growing UBI movement. We are in the midst of what I've elsewhere called the third wave of the UBI movement. The movement has been sparked by at least a dozen different sources. Its growth is closely related to growing dissatisfaction with inequality, poverty, and existing policies to deal with them, all of which have greatly increased since the financial crisis of 2008–2009.[1]

Trials are a strange response to a movement made up almost entirely of people who are already convinced UBI works and who want it introduced. There is no movement of people who are simply curious about UBI's effects and who would like to examine the particular effects that trials are capable of examining.

Therefore, the value UBI experiments to UBI supporters is their strategic value. That is, they might help build support for UBI and eventually lead to its introduction. To say that trials are happening for strategic reasons is not to say that UBI supporters want anything less than a good, evidence-based study. The strategic hope is that scientific inquiry into the issue will demonstrate the efficacy of the program, attract positive attention, build the movement, and lead to its introduction.

Yet the strategic hope for experiments can overshadow concern about the experiment itself. People rarely say anything to the effect of "we want an experiment because it is a particularly good way to examine aspect X of the UBI issue." People more often say simply that "we want a UBI experiment," without any connection between it and any particular thing one might want to learn from it.

Trials do have great promise, but they are a risky strategy for the UBI movement and are controversial among UBI supporters. Why then are so many policymakers around the world suddenly so interested in experiments? Consider five possible reasons. This list is not exhaustive and will not apply in all circumstances.

[1] Widerquist, "Three Waves of Basic Income Support."

First (and least likely), a politician might support a trial to discredit the UBI movement. Although the results of a trial can be negatively spun, and some past experiments might have had negative effects on the movement, this motivation is extremely unlikely because it's too risky for politicians who oppose UBI. Just by supporting a trial, they risk alienating their UBI-opposing constituents. Just by talking about a trial they bring media attention to a policy they oppose. As the saying goes, there is no negative publicity. By conducting a trial, they commit years of funds to a strategy that might well backfire on them if they are unable to control how the trial is perceived. Any UBI opponent with the power to use such an elaborate strategy to discredit UBI is probably better off using that power to keep UBI out of the mainstream dialogue: an experiment would sabotage that effort, keeping UBI on the table for years.

Second, politicians, along with policy wonks in academia or in government service, might institute an experiment to examine a narrow range of technical issues about UBI or about small steps in the direction of unconditionality. Although this might be an important motivation for some experiments, I do not dwell on it here, having discussed it in the introduction.

Third, politicians might be driven by pure scientific curiosity. UBI is hotly debated partly because its effects are controversial. A trial can help resolve some of that controversy and enlighten the discussion while promoting science. This motivation isn't terribly likely in most cases. Probably, most politicians are politicized. If they are going to support a trial, they have some partisan interest in the outcome of a trial or at least an interest in the constituency demanding the trial. This might be less true in the Netherlands, where municipalities were given latitude to experiment, but even with such latitude, policymakers will probably try things that interest them and their constituents.

Fourth, politicians might support UBI and believe that a trial will ultimately be good for the movement. If there are enough committed UBI supporters in government to pass a law instituting a trial of UBI, why don't they just skip the trial and pass a law introducing a full UBI right away? UBI is no small idea. Virtually any substantial version of BIG would be an enormous change to any country's public policy system. Despite the UBI movement's growth, the idea is still a minority opinion in most countries. It would be an enormous risk for politicians to make such a change without the confidence that they had a substantial constituency behind them. Politicians might hope that a successful trial can help build that coalition, and so the politicians opting for a trial rather than the immediate introduction of UBI might nevertheless share some of the motivations of UBI supporters.[2]

Fifth, a trial could be some kind of consolation prize for the UBI movement. While the UBI movement wants the support of politicians, politicians want the support of the UBI movement. A consolation prize could be politicians' way of saying that the movement has grown enough to be taken seriously and enough that at least some political parties find it useful to seek the support of that movement. But the constituency has not grown enough to demand full introduction of UBI in exchange for that support. The consolation prize of a UBI experiment may be the next best politically feasible thing that politicians can do at this point to get the UBI movement to support them.

Politicians have a massive incentive to find *the cheapest way to tell you yes.* Even the most well-meaning politicians might feel some of the pressure of the political incentive structure that pushes in this direction. They might *want* to support the UBI movement's cause (full implementation), but they *need* to get the UBI movement to support their cause (reelection). The enormous difference in cost (both monetary and political) between a UBI trial and actual implementation makes it far easier for a politician to deliver a trial. From the politicians' perspective, this is a triple win: they gain a constituency, support scientific research, and take action that might someday lead to the introduction of a policy they sympathize with (i.e. a mix of the third, fourth, and fifth reasons to favor trials). Politicians might not be fully aware of the extent to which they are affected by each of these motivations.

A danger for the UBI movement comes along with this possible mix of motivations: trials might end up deflecting political momentum away from full implementation of UBI. Once a trial is in place, it can become a temporary barrier to full implementation. A good trial can last 3–7 years or more from inception to final report. Having said *yes* to a trial, the politician now has the perfect excuse to say *no* to implementation for that entire period. You asked for a trial; I gave it to you; it only makes sense to wait to fully evaluate the findings of the trial you wanted before taking the next

[2] However, they might not share the same vision of UBI. Therefore, similarity in motive doesn't imply that they will test the same version of UBI that supporters are most interested in. A UBI test cannot be as diverse as the UBI movement is.

step. Three-to-seven years is a long time in politics. The movement could peak during that period. Sympathetic parties could lose power. The unfinished NIT experiments might well have been a barrier to the introduction of some form of BIG in the United States when a bill was active in Congress in 1971 and 1972.

Having discussed the social and political process of bringing experiments about, the next chapter discusses the social and political reaction to experimental results.

CHAPTER 10

The Vulnerability of Experimental Findings to Misunderstanding, Misuse, Spin, and the Streetlight Effect

Abstract This chapter examines why the results of basic income experiments are so easily misunderstood, and, therefore, vulnerable to spin, sensationalism, and other forms of misuse. These problems exist because of the inherent complexity of the material, the differences in background knowledge of the people involved, and the political nature of the issue.

Keywords Basic income experiments • Negative Income Tax experiments • Social science experiments • Basic income • Universal Basic Income • Inequality • Poverty

This chapter attempts to help anyone involved in the discussion of the current round of experiments to avoid misunderstanding, misuse, spin, and the streetlight effect by explaining why UBI experiments are so vulnerable to those problems. Misunderstandings happen because the nonspecialists who create the demand for experiments and the specialists who conduct the experiments have great difficulty understanding each other, and they are separated by a long and difficult chain of connections. Essentially, we're playing the telephone game, in which one person tells another person a story; the second person passes it to a third, and so on. Each degree of separation adds potential for misunderstanding, and the story gets less and less accurate the more it is passed on.

K. Widerquist, *A Critical Analysis of Basic Income Experiments for Researchers, Policymakers, and Citizens*, Exploring the Basic Income Guarantee, https://doi.org/10.1007/978-3-030-03849-6_10

The telephone game is especially difficult for UBI experiments because we're playing it with inherently difficult information, and the people involved don't always have a shared set of background assumptions. All research—any discussion—involves background assumptions, but when information moves from groups with differing sets of background assumptions, misunderstandings creep in.

It's common but wrong to distract attention from background assumptions as if they were unchallengeable truths. People do this both consciously and unconsciously. Even if people explain them, background assumptions are easily lost because they're not the most interesting part of the story to pass along to the next person. A lack of understanding about the background assumptions that go into research can lead to the impression that it is more definitive than it actually is.

Consider how the chain of connections affects UBI experiments. The citizens who create the demand for trials might not know what questions experiments can and cannot address. I've argued that most citizens are interested in the big questions, an overall verdict on UBI's efficacy. They will probably count on researchers conducting studies to decide what questions to address and how to address them, and they might presume or at least hope that these experts will be able to anticipate the questions they want answered and translate that evidence into the right answers.

Politicians, rather than the people most closely involved in the UBI discussion, usually make the decision to have a trial. Only a few of them will be closely connected to that discussion. They might be interested in a different definition of UBI than the one used by most supporters. Whatever UBI model politicians decide to test, they cannot be counted on to know what questions are most relevant to the citizens involved on any side of the public discussion. Often, they seem to have no specific questions in mind, and when they do, their questions might differ from the questions most important to the public discussion.

Once politicians make the decision to have an experiment, they designate a government department to work on it. Appointed public servants in that department might in turn hire managers or consultants specifically for the project, and one of those groups appoints social scientists to design and conduct the study. These social scientists are, therefore, separated from the public discussion by several degrees, each of which has potential to add misunderstanding.

The researchers hired to conduct the trial might or might not be well-versed in the dialogue. There are researchers, like myself, who are heavily involved with the public discussion of UBI, but hiring those researchers increases the risk of confirmation bias. Researchers who are not involved in the UBI discussion will almost certainly research UBI as a policy, but they might not always research the public discussion of it or consult closely with people involved in that discussion. Although research will most likely be conducted by good scientists who will attempt to make a positive contribution to the body of knowledge about UBI, there are vulnerable to misunderstanding and likely to focus on aspects of the issue that depart substantially from the aspects that most interest people involved in the public discussion. Consider five reasons.

First, social scientists are not one united group with an automatically shared set of background assumptions. Specializations in many different fields and subfields are relevant to UBI and UBI experiments. Social scientists have to make an effort to develop a shared set of background assumptions across disciplinary barriers before they can develop a shared understanding with their nonspecialist audience.

Second, as discussed in the puzzle analogy in the introduction, social scientists tend to look at research questions very differently than nonspecialists. Nonspecialists tend to want a verdict, up or down. Social scientists know that no single study is very likely to produce a decisive verdict on any social science issue and tend to want to add to the existing body of knowledge about UBI.

Third, social scientists have no particular expertise in discovering the questions that concern others. Their expertise is in applying the tools they know to questions those tools are most suited to address. Politicians hired them, knowing their area of expertise is to conduct an experiment that can address some questions better than others. Social scientists might reasonably assume that they have been hired to do what they (and their experimental tools) do best. But, of course, the streetlight effect simply *is* the focus on what researchers and/or experiments do best instead of the questions that most need to be answered.

Fourth, social scientists have a strong interest in being seen by their peers as doing something *scientific*. The general climate in most of the social sciences is that quantitative research is somehow more scientific than qualitative research. Studies reporting numbers—the more quantifiable the better—are seen as more scientific than those reporting less quantifiable observations. In addition, RCTs are seen as being more scientific than saturation studies, even if a saturation study produces more relevant results to the issue being studied.

Fifth, specialists—like everyone else, including you and me—tend to have self-serving bias, in this case toward believing what they do is important. If so, they are likely to believe that whatever questions their experiment can address are more important than they actually are. They might underemphasize (to themselves and to others) the importance of all those questions that the experiments cannot address or the differences between experimental findings and their implications about the centrally important questions in the evaluation of UBI as a policy.

This analysis indicates the possibility that specialists conducting UBI experiments will be most interested in different questions than the nonspecialist citizens and policymakers involved in the discussion of UBI. This difference in concern would not be crucial if everyone understood it. Nonspecialists might be disappointed to learn the extent to which, instead of a decisive, overall evaluation of the policy, UBI experiments produced a small improvement in the existing knowledge about a few of the questions relevant to that overall evaluation, but as long as they learn enough about the research and its implications, research findings will improve their understanding of the evidence about UBI.

Unfortunately, the telephone game begins again as experimental findings make their way back into the public discussion.

Researchers usually take other researchers as their primary audience. When they do, they write in the exacting academic terms familiar to other researchers and leave out the background knowledge familiar to other researchers in their respective fields but not necessarily familiar to people outside of their field. As Chap. 1 mentioned, many excellent researchers are not very good at communicating with nonspecialists.

The US and Canadian experiments released findings in the 1970s and early 1980s mostly in specialist-to-specialist publications, such as academic monographs and journals,[1] which are dense and difficult for nonspecialists.

Hopefully, the new round of studies will produce at least some reports aimed at general audiences. They might even employ science communication specialists to report the results in language that nonspecialists can best understand. However, even the best-written reports might not attempt to bridge the most important gaps in understanding. Research reports often aim to help nonspecialists understand scientific findings *on their own terms* more than they aim to help relate those findings to the questions that most

[1] Karl Widerquist, "The Bottom Line in a Basic Income Experiment," *Basic Income Studies* 1, no. 2 (2006).

concern nonspecialists. For example, reports might help people understand how the behavior of the control group differed from the behavior of the experimental group in the ways that researchers were capable of studying. For at least four reasons, reports might not attempt the very complex and difficult effort required to explain how much (and how little) these differences say about the likely overall effects of a national UBI in the areas of most concern to nonspecialists.

First, it's not necessarily their job. Unless specifically instructed, it is not usually the job of researchers or of science communication specialists to find out what questions interest other people. Their job is to conduct research and explain the findings of that research. If our political process hires specialists to do job A, we cannot blame them for neglecting our unspoken need for them to do job B as well.

Second, what is obvious to specialists is not always obvious to nonspecialists, who share few background assumptions with specialists. These studies are short term. They do not capture community effects. They produce indirect and partial inferences about the national implementation of a policy. They do not address all of the important claims needed to fully evaluate UBI as a policy. From one specialist to another this list might seem too obvious to mention, or it might seem to merit no more than a dry list of caveats so that other specialists know that the researchers conducting the study were aware of these limitations. If specialists are unaware how poorly nonspecialists understand these issues, they might not even mention them, much less work through the difficult effort needed to connect experimental results to the questions nonspecialists want answered.

Third, self-serving comes into play again. We all tend to believe what we do is important. A report emphasizing all the barriers between the experimental results and the things we really want to know would make the experiments look less valuable than they would look in a report that ignored or downplayed those differences. Similarly, a report emphasizing how much theory and data from other sources were necessary to connect the experimental results to the evaluation of the actual effects of a national policy would make the experiments themselves look less valuable.

Fourth, the pressure for social scientists to be seen doing something scientific (often conflated with doing something quantitative) also comes into play again. The effort to discuss the limitations of experimental findings in order to connect them with answers to the questions nonspecialists most want answered will involve doing more qualitative and nonacademic discussion.

Whether for these reasons or others reports about the US experiments in the 1970s overwhelmingly stressed the differences between the behavior of the control and experimental groups rather than the part these play in understanding how to evaluate BIG as a potential national policy.[2]

Even if research reports do address the big questions that most concern nonspecialists, the effort to help create a good, shared understanding will be difficult. No matter how well-written reports might be, they face the inherent problem that the information they contain is complex and difficult. After all, any nonspecialist who learns what specialists know becomes a specialist. Some amount of the complex implications of a UBI trial simply will be missed by most nonspecialists. The trick is to get them to understand *enough*. That task is not usually impossible, but it is seldom easy. Weeding through the complexity of the issue to determine what is enough and figuring out how to communicate it is intrinsically difficult.

People reading about UBI experiments might be biased toward oversimplification just because they're looking for something they can understand. They also might be biased in this direction by what we might call "professional deference." By this, I mean the mistaken belief that expert findings are more definitive than even the specialists themselves believe. In everyday conversations, if one person says several negative things about an idea, they are implying that the idea itself is bad and should be rejected. Research reports by contrast are to be taken at face value. If they don't include statements about the big questions, that means they don't have answers to those questions. Unfortunately, not all readers will understand that. At least some of them will probably take every positive-sounding result as the experts' vote for and every negative-sounding result as the experts' vote against the policy. Even a clear caveat warning readers against making such inferences might be ignored by some readers or journalists.

Whether or not researchers conducting experiments produce reports attempting to explain that complexity directly to nonspecialists, most nonspecialists (i.e. most citizens and politicians) will get their information about the study not from research reports but from popular writers, such as journalists, bloggers, and columnists,[3] creating yet another degree of separation, and one that involves opportunities for spin and sensationalism.

[2] Ibid.

[3] I use "popular writers" to mean people who write for nonspecialists (the populace), not to mean people who have a lot of readers.

Popular writers might well be professional writers, but few of them are professional social scientists. Only a few of them will have much more expertise than the public they write for. They might struggle to understand research reports even on their own terms. They might be incapable of doing the complex analysis necessary to relate reported differences between the control and experimental groups to probable outcomes for a national UBI. That is, they might have some of the same problems as their readers in understanding the results of UBI trials.

Popular writers, especially if their understanding is limited or oversimplified, are likely to be biased toward sensationalism. The reporting in the 1970s on the NIT experiments was overwhelmingly sensational.[4] Whether it is out of professional deference, a desire to attract more readers or the inherent difficulty of the material, many recent reports about the UBI experiments getting underway now have been sensational.[5] For example, Matt Reynolds recently debunked a significant amount of sensational reports saying that Finland *cancelled* its UBI experiment, when it simply decided *not to extend* the experiment.[6]

Most likely, some writers, politicians, and even some researchers will—consciously or unconsciously—spin the results to the advantage of one side or other in the debate. "Spin"—as I use the term—is not necessarily deceptive. To spin is to present information in a way that favors one or another interpretation of it. A person (like me) who is convinced UBI is a good idea cannot present what they know honestly without also putting UBI in a favorable light. The same is true for opponents. Honest spin is not unethical, but it is a source of misunderstanding as information goes through the telephone game.

Spin becomes dishonest when people knowingly overemphasize one side of the issue over another. This kind of spin can still be unconscious if it stems from a bias toward recognizing favorable evidence as more important than unfavorable evidence, but it is deceptive and can be a big source of misunderstanding. Spin becomes extreme when people look at evidence not as a way to improve their understanding but as a source of ammunition to use to defend their preconceived position.

[4] Widerquist, "The Bottom Line in a Basic Income Experiment."

[5] Kristin Houser and June Javelosa, "Bill Gates: The World Isn't Ready for Universal Basic Income Now, but We Will Be Soon," Futurism.com, February 28, 2017; Condliffe.

[6] Matt Reynolds, "No, Finland Isn't Scrapping Its Universal Basic Income Experiment," *Wired*, April 26, 2018.

Most citizens will get their information from popular articles. As those citizens absorb that information, they add another degree of separation to the telephone game. They might add a layer of misunderstanding or oversimplification to what might already exist in the article.

All this adds up to a great danger that even well-conducted experiments will fail to increase the understanding of evidence among people engaged in the public debate. This risk doesn't require any of the people involved to be fools or fakers; this risk exists because a lot of people are involved in a long chain of transmission of very complex information, about which they share few background assumptions. I've argued that communication problems like these had a detrimental effect on the discussion of the NIT experiments in the 1970s. It's important not to let that happen to the current round of UBI experiments.

1 Working Backward from the Public Discussion and Forward to It Again

I'll put off most of the discussion of how to combat misunderstanding, misuse, spin, and sensationalism until the concluding chapter. But I will say one thing now. People commissioning, designing, and conducting UBI experiments should work backward from an understanding of the public discussion to the experiment by identifying the claims that are important to the public discussion and attempting to relate all their findings to those claims. Then, they should work forward again, explaining the relevance of the experimental findings to the issues that are important to the discussion.

Working backward from the debate does not require experiments to test everything everyone wants to know about UBI. It requires researchers to try their best to identify the questions that interest the public, especially the big bottom-line questions, and relate the things they can find to the issues that are most valuable to the public evaluation of UBI as a policy. Not only can this effort help researchers design experiments that are better understood, but it will also help them design experiments that are more genuinely useful to the public decision of whether to introduce UBI.

Once the experiment is complete, researchers and others writing about experiments should work forward again from the test to the public discussion, explaining carefully what the experiments findings do and do not imply about the issues of interest to the public discussion of UBI. This effort involves calling attention to the limits of experiments, and it might, therefore, make the experiments seem less valuable. But a good understanding of what experiments cannot do is essential to the understanding of what they can do.

The next seven chapters consider the process of working backward from the debate to the design of the experiment. It's a daunting but worthwhile task.

CHAPTER 11

Why UBI Experiments Cannot Resolve Much of the Public Disagreement About UBI

Abstract This chapter explains why Universal Basic Income (UBI) experiments cannot resolve the public disagreement about UBI. It argues not only that experiments make a small contribution to the large body of available evidence, but also that the discussion turns less on remaining unknowns about UBI's effects than on the ethical desirability of UBI's known effects.

Keywords Basic income experiments • Negative Income Tax experiments • Social science experiments • Basic income • Universal Basic Income • Inequality • Poverty

The belief that a UBI experiment can provide a definitive answer to the question of whether to introduce UBI rests on three false presumptions: (1) People disagree about UBI primarily because they disagree about what its effects might be. (2) These disagreements about effects stem from a lack of available evidence. (3) An experiment will provide that missing evidence.

In each case, nearly the opposite is true: (1) Although some important disagreements about UBI's effects exists, the disagreement is more of an ethical debate about the desirability of its effects than an empirical debate about what those effects are. (2) Disagreements about what UBI's effects

K. Widerquist, *A Critical Analysis of Basic Income Experiments for Researchers, Policymakers, and Citizens*, Exploring the Basic Income Guarantee, https://doi.org/10.1007/978-3-030-03849-6_11

are don't stem primarily from a lack of available evidence. Substantial evidence already exists. Some of it is widely known; some isn't. (3) Experiments cannot provide the most important missing evidence. They will only add a small amount to the existing body of evidence and leave many important empirical questions about UBI unanswered.

Therefore, this chapter explores the difference between the questions that need to be resolved to make a decision for or against UBI and the answers UBI experiments can provide. The difference is bound to disappoint some readers, and some might react by saying why bother (see Chap. 18), but it's necessary to understand what an experiment's limits are if we're going to get the most out of it.

Experiments are empirical studies. They can provide evidence to help answer empirical questions like, *what does this do?* But they cannot provide the answer to ethical and subjective questions, such as *do we want what this does?* Experiments cannot resolve the basic disagreement, which is more about the second question than the first. The focus on ethics is not because people don't care about evidence, but as argued below, because UBI's likely effects are well-enough understood and the moral desirability of those effects is controversial enough to make the ethical part of the argument pivotal.

For example, UBI supporters tend to believe either (1) that it is good for everyone to be free from the threat of poverty, including nonwealthy people who might refuse to take jobs, or (2) that the possibility of nonwealthy people refusing to take jobs is not bad enough to compel sacrificing other goals that UBI achieves. Opponents tend to believe it is wrong for anyone (who isn't independently wealthy) to get anything without taking a job. These positions differ on basic ethical premises—as do positions in many similar disagreements over UBI. No empirical study of the practical effects of a UBI will determine whether these two incompatible ethical beliefs are right or wrong.

Although there are many nonethical reasons to support or oppose UBI, this ethical divide exists in the background of most discussions over UBI's ability to achieve its goals. People who haven't made up their minds on UBI often bring up concerns that are closely related to this and similar ethical disputes.

This aspect of the UBI discussion makes it very different from the climate change discussion. One reason the denial of evidence plays such a large role in the climate change debate is that if climate change *is* happening, it seems obvious we should do something about it. Therefore, those who don't want to do anything about it feel they have to get people to believe it is not happening. By contrast, it is entirely possible for two people to agree about all the effects of UBI and disagree about whether it is a good policy. People on one side of the issue or the other do not necessarily have to deny any evidence to make their case for or against the policy.

Empirical research can find evidence that is useful to people discussing ethical issues. For example, if research was to find out that people with UBI tend to make as good or better contributions to society as people do without UBI, at least some people who are leery about allowing nonwealthy people to live without taking a job would probably become more open to UBI. But not all people who oppose UBI for this kind of reason will be swayed. Some might believe nonwealthy people need to work more than they are working now. Others might oppose UBI because they oppose even the possibility that a nonwealthy person might refuse to participate in the labor market.

Similarly, if empirical research found that a given level of UBI caused a decrease in employment so large that it threatened UBI's sustainability, any UBI supporters who aren't extremely short-sighted would drop their support for UBI or at least for that level of UBI if they were unable to suggest a policy to counteract that unsustainability.

Yet, experiments in wealthy countries are unlikely to show either result. Past evidence strongly indicates that low-wage workers in wealthy countries will spend less time in employment, but not so much less that UBI will become unsustainable. If experiments are consistent with a decline in labor hours in that range, supporters are likely to say UBI passed the test and opponents are likely to say that it failed. People whose opinions are in the middle might be swayed by where in that range the estimate falls, but a subtle finding like this isn't likely to be a huge deviation from what we can already estimate from existing evidence. And it's possible that responses of people in the middle will be affected less by the small amount of additional evidence than by who wins the spin wars that are likely to follow the release of experimental findings.

Closely related to the issue of whether empirical findings can resolve the ethical debate over UBI is the problem of separating empirical from ethical claims about UBI. Almost any social policy study has to deal with the problem that it is not easy to evaluate whether the policy "works" without making ethical judgments about how to evaluate performance. We can say empirically whether UBI meets criterion X, but we have to make an ethical judgment to say how important X is as a criterion (see Chap. 12).

An enormous amount of evidence about UBI's effects already exists. Thousands of articles and books on various aspects of its effects have been written and seven large-scale trials conducted worldwide between 1968 and 2013. In addition, studies of full-fledged policies of varying degrees of similarity to UBI, such as the Alaska Dividend, conditional cash transfers, citizens' pensions, tax credits, and many others, provide information that can be used to estimate UBI's effects.[1]

My impression—after studying UBI for more than 20 years—is that the better one grasps existing evidence, the more likely one's decision comes down to ethical issues. I can say that the right UBI scheme will be sustainable and will do things people with an ethical position similar to mine want it to do, but it will also do things that people with different ethical positions do not want it to do.

Although many reasonable people are in the middle and might well be swayed by new evidence, many people in the middle aren't familiar with the existing evidence, and it is uncertain that a new experiment will provide the most important piece of missing evidence they have been looking for.

Existing evidence is not assembled in any one spot nor is most of it easily accessible to nonspecialists. The most accessible summaries of existing evidence are in books written by supporters such as Annie Miller, Guy Standing, Malcolm Torry, Philippe Van Parijs, Yannick Vanderborght, and others.[2] Of course, books by supporters might be subject to confirmation bias.

Despite the enormous amount of evidence available in the relevant social science literature and the availability of good summaries, a substantial part of the current discussion of UBI among citizens and policymakers still goes on in ignorance of existing evidence. In fact, a lot of clearly false claims easily contradicted by evidence are regularly repeated in the debate. For example, many people continue to claim that a poverty-level UBI would cost 15–20% of gross domestic product (GDP), when the actual

[1] Widerquist and Howard, *Alaska's Permanent Fund Dividend: Examining Its Suitability as a Model*; *Exporting the Alaska Model: Adapting the Permanent Fund Dividend for Reform around the World*; Joseph Hanlon, Armando Barrientos, and David Hulme, *Just Give Money to the Poor: The Development Revolution from the Global South* (Boulder, CO: Kumarian Press, 2010); Guy Standing, "How Cash Transfers Promote the Case for Basic Income," *Basic Income Studies* 3, no. 1 (2008).

[2] Annie Miller, *A Basic Income Handbook* (Edinburgh: Luath Press Limited, 2017); Guy Standing, *Basic Income: And How We Can Make It Happen* (New York: Penguin, 2017); Van Parijs and Vanderborght; Karl Widerquist et al., *Basic Income: An Anthology of Contemporary Research* (Oxford: Wiley-Blackwell, 2013); Malcolm Torry, *The Feasibility of Citizen's Income* (New York: Palgrave Macmillan, 2016).

amount is estimated to be about one-sixth of that figure, less than 3% of GDP.[3] Future discussions might go on in ignorance of most of the findings of the current round of experiments.

Important gaps in existing evidence do remain. Experiments can help fill in some of those gaps, but as following chapters discuss, experiments are only capable of testing a small subset of what we really want to know about UBI. And many of the biggest and most important gaps in the existing evidence are not things that UBI experiments are capable of addressing. Neither these gaps nor the potential for UBI experiments to fill them in are well-understood by nonspecialists, including some of the reporters currently writing about the experiments.

The decision to conduct a UBI experiment should be made with full knowledge of all these limitations. If we want a UBI experiment, we need to accept not only that it is incapable of settling the major ethical divides between supporters and opponents, and that it is highly unlikely to prove either of their positions untenable, but also that it is unlikely to provide a large enough addition to existing evidence to give a compelling reason for massive numbers of people in the middle to shift their opinions significantly. Like most social science research projects, UBI experiments will make an incremental contribution to existing evidence. If the results are well-communicated, their best realistic hope is to enlighten the discussion among people on all sides of the current discussion by increasing both the evidence available to them and their understanding of it. This is a good reason to do an experiment, but it is far short of the definitive test people want and some seem to be expecting.

I suspect that some specialists will mistakenly believe that everything this chapter says is too obvious to mention. That mistake is a central reason this book is necessary. Citizens and policymakers have to be free of false hopes if their decision to conduct a UBI experiments is to be based on what an experiment can actually do.

[3] Widerquist, "The Cost of Basic Income: Back-of-the-Envelope Calculations."

CHAPTER 12

The Bottom Line

Abstract This chapter discusses how people that are designing and conducting experiments can work backward from the claims important to the public discussion of Universal Basic Income (UBI) to the claims experiments are able to examine. It suggests that UBI experiments should relate all findings to what it calls "the bottom line": an overall assessment of the cost-effectiveness of a fully implemented national UBI. An issue-specific bottom line for any variable of interest should also be considered. Experiments cannot answer the bottom-line questions, but experimental reports can explain how their findings relate to those questions.

Keywords Basic income experiments • Negative Income Tax experiments • Social science experiments • Basic income • Universal Basic Income • Inequality • Poverty

The "bottom line" is the central question in any policy debate: an overall evaluation of that policy in both empirical and ethical terms. Does it work? Should we do it? Because experiments can't address ethical questions, researchers will have to focus on the does-it-work question in light of the ethical issues also under discussion. This chapter attempts to identify an overall bottom-line question and to understand how to frame smaller bottom-line questions for specific issues. The following chapter goes on to

K. Widerquist, *A Critical Analysis of Basic Income Experiments for Researchers, Policymakers, and Citizens*, Exploring the Basic Income Guarantee, https://doi.org/10.1007/978-3-030-03849-6_12

identify more-specific claims that are important to the discussion, setting up the subsequent discussion of the extent to which experiments can directly or indirectly address each of those claims.

1 Identifying and Overall Bottom Line

Identifying the bottom line is more difficult than it might appear. The question *does UBI work* is too vague for a social science experiment, partly because whether something "works" depends on controversial ethical questions such as what goals it is supposed to accomplish and how tolerable are potential side effects. Social scientists tend to translate the does-it-work question into the cost-effectiveness question: how cost-effective is it? This question sounds very scientific and neutral, but it still requires a resolution to controversial ethical questions. Which effects of UBI morally count as costs? Which count as benefits? What relative weights do we put on benefits X, Y, and Z and on costs A, B, and C? Whether something (such as a decline in average labor hours among low-wage workers) is considered a negative "side effect" or a positive "effect" often depends on controversial ethical issues. If citizens and policymakers could resolve all of these issues and hand empirical researchers an index to weigh costs and benefits, researchers would have a purely empirical question to examine. But no one can resolve these deep moral controversies in advance of a study.

Empirical researchers are, therefore, forced to impose some controversial judgments on their evaluation process. They should warn readers what these judgments are in an attempt to create a shared set of background assumptions. But doing so can sound as if it merely adds yet another caveat. Perhaps, they should go farther and examine several different moral weighting systems to provide information for people with differing ethical positions.

Empirical economists sometimes ignore ethical background assumptions in their evaluative tools. Many economists look at costs exclusively in dollar terms and cast cost-benefit calculations in efficiency terms, with little or no discussion of the debate over whether these measures should have ethical priority over other options. For example, although a dollar lost to anyone is an efficiency loss, citizens might have good ethical reasons to value a dollar used to cure poverty more than several dollars used to provide luxuries for the already wealthy.[1]

[1] Similarly, people with differing ethical beliefs might give a higher moral priority to a less efficient system that forced nonwealthy people to accept employment than to a more efficient redistribution system that gave them the opportunity to refuse employment.

In the absence of a national resolution to the ethical controversies that create this problem, researchers will have to impose something, but they should avoid presenting their resolution to moral issues as if it were uncontroversial. It is better to be open about the moral judgments necessary to frame the empirical issues. It's also valuable to recognize the different moral perspectives that are relevant in the local political context and present evaluations relevant to each. This book cannot resolve this issue and won't dwell on it.

I attempt to state the cost-effectiveness question in broad terms as:

> Is a fully implemented national UBI a cost-effective method to benefit people in the short and long run in the ways UBI supporters claim it does, assuming cost-effectiveness is judged relative to other methods of achieving similar benefits for the same people?

Many of the things UBI supporters claim UBI can do (see Chap. 13) require a generous UBI in the context of an extensive welfare system doing the things UBI cannot do. Although some aspects of the welfare system can be replaced by UBI (most notably policies designed to maintain the incomes to a level sufficient for normally abled people), other aspects are not so replaceable. Exactly what that extensive welfare system should involve is controversial even among UBI supporters, but it might include education, healthcare, childcare, eldercare, disability care, a higher-than-basic income for people with greater-than-normal needs, family leave, infrastructure, transportation, public safety, an affordable housing policy, and so on.

Testing a full UBI in that context might not be possible, and it is reasonable for researchers to test only a small step in the direction of UBI supporters' vision. But, if we test only that step, we are not testing the UBI that inspired the movement. Sometimes small steps work when big leaps fail (such as toward the end of a dock). Sometimes big leaps work when small steps fail (such as over a ditch). Whatever version of UBI (or whatever UBI-like policy) we test, researchers should clearly explain how it differs from other versions and the extent to which this test's findings do or do not have implications for other versions of UBI.

It might, therefore, be useful in some circumstances to state the bottom-line question in slightly more incremental terms:

> What policy (basic income, the current system, or any other alternatives to be tested) produces the greatest increase in recipients' welfare per unit of cost (both in terms of tax cost and efficiency loss), in the context of a long-term, fully implemented national policy?[2]

Obviously, these statements of the bottom line can be shortened if some of their constraining phrases can go without saying. I hesitate to do so because of the amount of misunderstanding these issues have caused in the past.

I suggest that one of these cost-benefit questions—or something like them—should be considered the bottom line for UBI experiments. Experimental evidence cannot definitively answer the bottom-line question, but experimenters can relate experimental findings to it: how does this research improve our understanding of the bottom line?

These specifications of the bottom line impose answers to some moral questions. I've tried to reduce this problem by phrasing the question in relative terms—relative to supporters' claims about its benefits and relative to other ways of achieving those benefits. It intentionally leaves open what the claimed costs and benefits are.

I'm concerned with overidentifying any claim as "the" goal of UBI in any political context. The UBI movement is diverse, as is the opposition to UBI. Some see UBI as a way to eliminate the threat of poverty for everyone. Some see it as a way to make alternative lifestyles possible. Some see it as a way to simplify and streamline the tax and benefit system. And so on. I doubt there is any political context in which virtually everyone who discusses UBI is interested only in a very limited range of issues.

Phrasing the cost-effectiveness question in relative terms does not eliminate moral controversies. For example, even if nearly everyone might agree that a central goal of UBI is to "increase recipients' welfare" (as used above), any effort to define "welfare" is controversial. Popular welfare measures might leave out some of the concerns that are important to the UBI discussion. Researchers should not simply stop using these measures, but they can supplement them by discussion of how UBI affects important items that can't be incorporated into the index.

The important points are not that the bottom line is phrased as I suggest, but that the experiments have a bottom line, that it is a broad question, that it compares costs and benefits, that it refrains from distracting

[2] Widerquist, "The Bottom Line in a Basic Income Experiment."

attention from things experiments cannot measure, and that it addresses what people need and want to know to evaluate UBI as a potential policy in their country or region.

The overall bottom line is important for two reasons. First, virtually any empirical research question can and should be understood as some part of the answer to this general question. Second, it is what citizens and policymakers ultimately need or want to learn from empirical policy research. The more they know about the cost-effectiveness of UBI, the more fully informed they will be as they discuss and make the decision whether to implement UBI.

If citizens and policymakers believe many of the media reports on the launch of experiments, they not only want but *expect* a bottom-line answer. This expectation is an important reason to relate findings to the bottom line. Experiments have a much narrower objective. Experiments divide people into control and experimental groups, observe whatever differences they can, and test those differences for statistical significance. If experimental reports are limited to explaining what these differences are, they stop far short of any effort to find what people are looking for.

2 Issue-Specific Bottom Lines

Many issues can be usefully addressed in isolation. But no one has a direct interest in the simple comparison between the control and experimental groups for any observational variable. They have an interest in a long-term estimate for the impact of a national UBI on that variable. And they have an interest in viewing it in the context of cost-benefit analysis relative to other policies. Therefore, in addition to the overall bottom-line question, each variable can have a mini bottom line of its own. The bottom line for any particular variable is the cost-effectiveness of a long-term national UBI on that variable.

The calculation of the long-term impact of UBI on any variable involves considering community effects, the difference between a short-term study and a permanent policy, the ways in which the sample succeeds or fails to be representative of the entire population, and so on. For some variables, researchers might be able to use simulation techniques to calculate that answer. For others, they might have to bring in more qualitative information or simply have a qualitative discussion. Even if they lack data to make a reasonable estimate, they can explain the differences between what they found and what we really want to know. They can also discuss the missing factors necessary to get closer to the bottom line.

One example of an issue-specific bottom line is whether a step in the direction of universality can free people living on benefits from the poverty trap. This question, which seems to be important in the Finnish and Dutch experiments, is worth looking at even in isolation as long as the difference between it and an overall evaluation of UBI is clear.

Calculation of the overall bottom line requires a comparison of the bottom line for each particular variable estimated in the experiment and probably also with estimates for other variables the experiment could not examine. This effort, again, might be achieved with simulation techniques; it might instead require more qualitative techniques, or it might involve admitting why the effort falls short of that goal.

CHAPTER 13

Identifying Important Empirical Claims in the UBI Debate

Abstract This chapter proposes a list of important empirical claims made by supporters and opponents of Universal Basic Income (UBI) in an effort to identify what empirical questions UBI experiments should focus on and how researchers can relate experimental findings to the things people really want to know about UBI.

Keywords Basic income experiments • Negative Income Tax experiments • Social science experiments • Basic income • Universal Basic Income • Inequality • Poverty

This chapter presents two lists of claims that supporters and opponents have made about the effects of UBI. It gives each claim a name for reference, but these names do not reflect any standard definition. The list includes a definition for each claim, but little or no further discussion, such as how it is supposed to work. Later chapters give further explanations as needed.

I initially compiled this list by drawing on my own experience and then by using informal crowd sourcing, asking other people interested in UBI via social media whether they could contribute addition claims or rephrase some of the claims from my initial list. I have followed international news about UBI since 1999, and my contacts are largely international, but of course, my perspective still reflects my background. And so, the list reflects my biases.

K. Widerquist, *A Critical Analysis of Basic Income Experiments for Researchers, Policymakers, and Citizens*, Exploring the Basic Income Guarantee, https://doi.org/10.1007/978-3-030-03849-6_13

I have tried roughly to group similar claims together, going from the more common or important groups of claims to the less common or less important groups of claims, but the order is not terribly important. My estimates of how best to group claims and of the frequency and importance of claims are cursory and subjective. And of course, the importance of any claim varies substantially over time and place.

I have tried to reduce overlap as much as possible, but some overlapping claims play important, separate roles in the debate. Many claims could be divided into a series of more-specific claims. The welfare claim and the cost-effectiveness claim are obvious examples. Only some of the more-specific claims are included separately on the list; again, the criterion for including them separately was whether they play important independent roles in the UBI discussion.

It would be possible to include pairs of opposing claims on the supporters' list and the opponents' list: almost any claim on one list could be paired with its negation on the other list. For example, supporters tend to say UBI is cost-effective and affordable, while opponents tend to say it is cost-ineffective and unaffordable. I have tried to avoid these sorts of duplications by attributing it to the side that focuses on it more. Therefore, the supporters' list gets a cost-effectiveness claim and the opponents list gets an (un)affordability claim.

Although the lists don't include direct negations, they do include some pairs of opposite claims. For example, the benefit-to-workers claims and the harm-to-workers claims are included on the two lists because they play important separate roles in common arguments for and against. Many supporters don't stop at defending UBI against the allegation that it harms workers; they go on to argue about the ways in which UBI is likely to help many workers, and these arguments play an important role in their overall case for UBI.

Not all supporters or all opponents agree with each of the claims on the respective lists. In fact, some claims within each list contradict each other. This is to be expected, given that diverse people, sometimes with little else in common, support or oppose UBI for many different reasons.

These lists are not meant to exhaust all reasons given for or against UBI. No list could be. Based on my experience, however, they capture a large portion of the common and influential claims in the UBI literature. I expect that all or most of the questions experiments examine are related to some of the claims on these lists.

1 Claims Commonly Made by Supporters

The following list provides names for common claims supporters of UBI tend to make about its effects.

- The welfare claim: UBI significantly raises the welfare of net recipients and some net contributors.
- The poverty claim: UBI (usually in combination with other policies) can eliminate poverty.
- The structural-disadvantage (or economic-and-social-mobility) claim: UBI increases economic and social mobility, and therefore reduces structural disadvantage by improving the health, security, and education of children, and by helping adults start businesses, get education or training, take the time to look for the right job, and in many other ways.
- The economic-equality claim: UBI increases economic equality both by direct redistribution to lower-income people and by indirect effects, such as creating more favorable labor-market conditions, improving health, and increasing education. (The taxes used to support it can also be formulated to increase equality.)
- The social-equality (or social-inclusion) claim: UBI increases social equality by reducing social isolation of low-income people, by reducing the stigmatization of people who benefit from redistributive programs, by reducing housing segregation, and by other means.
- The benefit-to-workers claim: UBI financially benefits many workers directly by acting as a wage subsidy for lower-income workers and indirectly by creating market conditions likely to increase wages.
- The better-working-conditions claim: UBI improves working conditions both by giving workers the flexibility to move to more attractive sectors and by creating market conditions likely to cause conditions to improve.
- The widespread-benefit claim: a large portion of the population will benefit (on average) from UBI at any one time, and a substantially larger portion will benefit at some point in their lives.
- The flexible-lifestyle claim: UBI enables people to work shorter hours, engage in job sharing, become full-time parents, and so on.
- The freedom claim: UBI gives people greater freedom in the sense of giving them more effective power over their own lives by reducing or eliminating their dependence on employers.

- The compensation claim: those who own resources owe a UBI to those who do not in compensation for the unequal division of the world's resources.
- The anti-exploitation claim: UBI reduces exploitation in employment by giving all workers (both inside and outside unions) the power to refuse exploitive working conditions.
- The cost-effectiveness claim: UBI is more cost-effective than traditional, conditional welfare policies (in achieving various goals).
- The reduced-social-costs claim: by reducing poverty and inequality, UBI reduces associated costs such as healthcare, policing, and so on.
- The reduced-capture-corruption-and-bureaucracy claim(s): UBI's benefits are less likely to be captured by others (such as employers, landlords, and bureaucrats) than conditional welfare state policies. And it is less vulnerable to corruption than conditional programs (because of its simplicity and transparency). These claims imply UBI reduces the overhead cost associated with income support.
- The efficient-transfer claim: UBI, being a lump-sum transfer, is economically efficient. The only social cost involved with it comes from increases in marginal tax rates associated with financing it, but not from the grant itself.
- The poverty-trap claim: UBI encourages people on benefits to reenter the labor force in greater numbers than a conditional system, by ensuring they are always better off earning more private income than earning less.
- The labor-productivity claim: UBI increases labor productivity by encouraging employers to substitute skilled for unskilled workers, by improving workers' ability to enhance their skills and search for higher-productivity jobs, and by improving childhood health and educational attainment.
- The increased-innovation-and-entrepreneurship claim: UBI increases entrepreneurial activity and innovation (because it increases the financial cushion for risk-takers and provides more time and more investment capital for visionaries to pursue ideas).
- The productive-nonlabor claim: UBI allows people to do more unpaid work (such as care work and volunteering), some of which is more productive (or socially valuable) than many forms of paid labor.
- The increased-support-for-redistribution claim: UBI, once in place, results in greater overall political support for redistribution.

- The politically-enabled-proletarian claim: UBI makes low-wage workers a greater force for progressive social change on other issues by freeing them from long hours and low pay.
- The economic-stimulus claim: UBI, in combination with the taxes that support it, helps improve economic growth and reduces unemployment by helping stimulate and stabilize aggregate demand.
- The "degrowth" claim: UBI helps economies move away from overconsumption and overexploitation of resources.
- The dynamic-efficiency claim: UBI increases the dynamic efficiency of the economy by increasing workers' health, education, safety, entrepreneurialism, and so on.

2 Claims Commonly Made by Opponents

The following list provides names for common claims opponents of UBI tend to make about its effects.

- The reciprocity (or work ethic) claim: UBI makes it possible for nonwealthy people to share in the benefits of social production, which involves labor, without making a reciprocal labor contribution of their own—or without any meaningful social contribution at all. This observation is often labeled a violation of norms such as reciprocity and/or the work ethic.
- The exploitation claim: UBI requires taxing workers for the benefit of nonworkers.
- The harm-to-workers claim: a UBI system financially benefits nonworkers at the expense of many workers, all effects considered.
- The labor-effort claim: UBI causes an unacceptably large reduction in labor supply that is not easily counteracted by other policies.
- The (un)affordability claim: UBI at the proposed level is prohibitively expensive.
- The economic-impediment claim: UBI decreases economic growth by various means, including reducing labor-market participation, increasing labor costs, causing inflation, creating the need for increased taxes, which reduces investment and innovation, and so on.
- The self-destruction claim: UBI increases self-destructive behavior (possibly including laziness, drug dependency, lack of care for the future, watching too much television, playing too many video games, choosing meaningless activities over meaningful paid work, having "too many" children, etc.).

- The gender-role-reinforcement claim: UBI helps maintain traditional gender roles by making it easier for women to remain out of the paid labor force while performing unpaid care work and other traditional women's roles.
- The consumerism claim: UBI, being a cash grant in a monetary economy, encourages greater consumerism, leading to increased environmental destruction and other problems.
- The bought-off-proletarian claim: UBI—by providing a minimal level of contentment for workers—reduces their effectiveness as a force to challenge the deeper inequalities and other social inequities in society.
- The decreased-overall-redistribution claim: UBI at an economically or politically feasible level makes low-income people worse off overall than traditional, conditional social policies.
- The capture claim: many of the benefits of UBI go to someone other than the recipients (perhaps because employers reduce wages, the cost of housing in low-income areas increases, bureaucrats create overhead costs, etc.).
- The migration claim: UBI encourages immigration and/or migration into areas with UBI.
- The shut-door claim: UBI creates political pressure to restrict immigration.

3 Conclusion

It's worth repeating that these lists are not exhaustive. Many more claims (of various levels of relevance, certainty, and testability) are undoubtedly circulating in the academic and nonacademic literature on UBI. But I hope these claims capture a significant range of what is being said. The diversity of claims on these lists is enough to demonstrate the difficulty of designing and communicating the results of a UBI experiment in a way that successfully enlightens the public discussion. The next three chapters consider how much an experiment can say about these claims and what research questions are useful to people interested in these claims.

CHAPTER 14

Claims That Don't Need a Test

Abstract This chapter identifies several empirical claims that should not be ignored by people designing, conducting, and writing about Universal Basic Income (UBI) experiments but that cannot be tested on an experimental scale. Evidence about these claims will have to come from other sources, which will have to be combined with experimental evidence to connect experimental findings to the most important questions for the public evaluation of UBI as a policy.

Keywords Basic income experiments • Negative Income Tax experiments • Social science experiments • Basic income • Universal Basic Income • Inequality • Poverty

At least five of the claims on the lists in Chap. 13 don't need a test to confirm their truth. Either they are true by definition or they can be shown to be true by analytical reasoning, with little or no empirical reasoning necessary. These include:

- The efficient-transfer claim
- The poverty claim
- The freedom claim
- The compensation claim
- The reciprocity (or work ethic) claim

K. Widerquist, *A Critical Analysis of Basic Income Experiments for Researchers, Policymakers, and Citizens*, Exploring the Basic Income Guarantee, https://doi.org/10.1007/978-3-030-03849-6_14

These claims are related to important claims that can be researched, and they can be used to help frame related research questions, but it is important to understand that they play a prominent role in the UBI discussion as stated—that is, as claims that are already verifiably true.

The efficient-transfer claim is analytically true. All lump-sum transfers are efficient in the sense defined by economists. That is, net recipients benefit financially as much as net taxpayers pay. Nonlump-sum transfers give individuals incentives to change their behavior to get the grant. These changes in behavior cause additional social costs. This fact has played a prominent role in the discussion among economists since James Buchanan, F.A. Hayek, and James Tobin endorsed the idea.

The efficiency claim applies to the grant, not necessarily the taxes used to support it. Lump-sum taxes, such as those on resource rents, are also efficient, and if UBI can be financed entirely by such taxes, no social cost would be involved with UBI at all. Experiments cannot test whether lump-sum taxes can raise enough revenue to support UBI, and experiments will probably assume that a substantial increase in nonlump-sum taxes will be necessary.

It is interesting the extent to which the discussion of UBI has ignored the efficient-transfer feature of UBI. The efficiency gain or loss of an economic policy proposal usually plays a large role in the academic discussion of it (and sometimes a role in the political discussion of it).

At least three research questions closely related to efficiency are important: first, what portion of UBI's cost represents an efficient transfer and what portion represents a social cost? Second, how does the efficiency loss of UBI in these terms compare to the efficiency loss of an equally generous expansion of existing programs? Third, to what extent do the dynamic-efficiency-improving effects of UBI (such as reducing the costs associated with poverty) counter the static inefficiency of the taxes needed to finance it?

These three questions have been neglected by most past experiments. The labor-market findings of UBI experiments will be useful toward answering these questions, but the experimental findings will have to be combined with a large amount of outside evidence to produce a result.[1] The need for evidence from other sources will be a running theme as these chapters try to relate the questions people want answered to the questions experiments can directly examine.

[1] See subsequent chapters.

The poverty claim, as stated, is analytically true. A UBI set at or above the poverty line necessarily eliminates poverty at least if poverty is defined in absolute terms. Relative poverty is trickier, because many UBI schemes will cause the median income to rise. For example, most European countries define the poverty line at 60% of median income. Eliminating poverty requires a UBI at 60% of the poverty line and a marginal tax rate of 60% for net recipients. Whether this UBI scheme is desirable and reasonably affordable is an open question, but whether it can be done is analytically true.

UBI's ability to *eliminate* poverty is an important advantage over the conditional approach, which necessarily leaves some portion of the population in poverty. If the people are truly required to meet conditions involved in nonuniversal approaches to poverty, a credible threat of poverty must exist, which would seem to require making good on that threat for at least some people. If so, conditional programs *have* to leave some people in both relative and absolute poverty. Yet, experiments can say nothing about this issue.

Several research questions related to poverty are relevant, such as what is the relative effectiveness of attempting to eliminate poverty with a UBI rather than by increasing existing transfer programs? And is a UBI that eliminates absolute or relative poverty affordable?

The freedom claim, **the compensation claim**, and **the reciprocity claim** are true by definition. The controversy is not over their truth but over their moral content. UBI set at a sufficient level undoubtedly gives nonwealthy people greater control over some aspects of their lives, increasing freedom in the sense used in the freedom claim. The same UBI can be considered compensation for the unequal division of resources. The same UBI makes it possible for nonwealthy people to consume products that involve labor without themselves contributing labor, violating the reciprocity principle in the sense used in that claim. No empirical investigation can settle the disagreement over the moral value of these senses of freedom and reciprocity.

There are important closely related empirical questions. The extent to which the benefit-to-workers claim, the productive-nonlabor claim, and the flexible-lifestyle claim hold true would indicate something about how valuable the added freedom for low-income people was, but unfortunately, UBI experiments are not the best way to investigate them (see below).

UBI experiments can contribute something to the question of whether more people violate this reciprocity principle under UBI, capitalism as is, or under an expanded conditional welfare system. However, to do so, they would have to define the ethically controversial concept of meaningful social contribution. Many people would object to whatever definition they chose.

One of the most valuable things researchers can do about the reciprocity issue is to head off the interpretation that experiments say more about it than they do. Experiments can and will certainly collect data on the labor time of the control and experimental groups. Opponents are likely to interpret any decline in labor time as an indication of a violation of the work ethic, and some writers are likely to spin it as such, as many did in the 1970s (see Chap. 6). Merely presenting labor-time findings—even on the way to calculating its effect on cost—without addressing its possible effect on the reciprocity principle invites that misconception among people for whom that principle is a primary concern.

To head off that mistake, researchers can address whether any labor-time decline reflects people dropping out of the labor force or merely reducing the number of hours they work. If researchers stop there, they leave open the interpretation that work is the only meaningful social contribution. But to go much further, they might have to define controversial moral claims. They can discuss the issue conceptually without getting into specific estimates of what should count, but some confusion on this issue might be inevitable.

Even if experiments could somehow show that UBI was very unlikely to cause an increase in violations of the politically relevant versions of the reciprocity principle, the truth that UBI makes it *possible* for nonwealthy people to live without laboring is likely still to feature prominently in the debate.

Some spin and some misunderstanding on all of these issues are inevitable. The goal is simply to reduce them as much as possible. To do so, anyone writing about experimental results needs to present them in a way that answers people's questions about how the findings relate to these issues. Few, if any, nonspecialists will be able to work out many of these issues for themselves, and they won't be helped much by a dry list of caveats.

CHAPTER 15

Claims That Can't Be Tested with Available Techniques

Abstract This chapter identifies several claims that are important to the public discussion and evaluation of Universal Basic Income (UBI) but that cannot be tested on an experimental scale. Unfortunately, for experimental research, these issues cannot be left out of the discussion of evidence about UBI. This chapter offers suggestions about how experimental reports should treat these questions to give people a good understanding of the meaning of experimental findings.

Keywords Basic income experiments • Negative Income Tax experiments • Social science experiments • Basic income • Universal Basic Income • Inequality • Poverty

This chapter discusses important empirical claims in the UBI discussion that are untestable or virtually untestable by the techniques available to potential UBI experiments, while Chap. 16 discusses claims that can be tested at least in some manner. That dichotomy is a simplification: in fact, there is a continuum between completely untestable and sufficiently testable claims, and it is a bit of a judgment call to determine which side of the line to put any particular claim. Tests will have *some* implications about most claims. The criteria that I've tried to use are whether the test can make some direct observations about the variable in question (as opposed

K. Widerquist, *A Critical Analysis of Basic Income Experiments for Researchers, Policymakers, and Citizens*, Exploring the Basic Income Guarantee, https://doi.org/10.1007/978-3-030-03849-6_15

to being connected by theory alone) and whether the theory connecting observations to the final effect on the variable is fairly settled and tends to point in one direction.

Experiments are virtually unable to test the following claims:

- The exploitation claim
- The anti-exploitation claim
- The social-equality claim
- The capture claim
- The reduced-capture-corruption-and-bureaucracy claim(s)
- The labor-productivity claim
- The increased-innovation-and-entrepreneurship claim
- The structural-disadvantage claim
- The better-working-conditions claim
- The flexible-lifestyle claim
- The productive nonlabor claim
- The gender-role-reinforcement claim
- The degrowth claim
- The consumerism claim
- The self-destruction claim
- The economic-stimulus claim
- The economic-impediment claim
- The migration claim
- The shut-door claim
- The increased-support-for-redistribution claim
- The increased-overall-disadvantage claim
- The politically-enabled-proletarian claim
- The bought-off-proletarian claim
- The dynamic-efficiency claim

The anti-exploitation claim and **the exploitation claim** are not polar opposites. The anti-exploitation claim involves UBI's suspected ability to reduce exploitation of workers by employers. The exploitation claim involves UBI's suspected ability to enable nonworking recipients to exploit workers. Depending on how exploitation is defined, it is possible for both claims to be true at the same time. A UBI could make workers less vulnerable to exploitation by employers while making them more vulnerable to exploitation for the benefit of nonworking net recipients. Similarly, the exploitation claim is distinct from the harm-to-workers claim. The exploitation claim focuses only on the effect of taxes. It is possible that some workers pay higher taxes under a UBI system, and so are exploited in the sense used, but are better off overall because of better wages and working conditions, as well as other community effects (see Chap. 16).

The concept of exploitation is so controversial and so morally loaded that researchers can't hope to say much about it directly, but it is so important that they should not ignore it either. They need to address other issues, such as the welfare claim, the benefit-to-workers claim, the better-working-conditions claim, and the harm-to-workers claim in the context of the exploitation debates. Unfortunately, these are difficult to address as well, as discussed in Chap. 16.

Despite the importance of **the social-equality claim**, experiments can say very little about it because it is inherently a community effect. Experiments will not directly reveal whether UBI net beneficiaries are less likely to be stigmatized than recipients of other redistributive programs. They won't observe housing segregation. Experimenters can ask people whether they feel socially isolated, but any relief from isolation is likely to be much larger in a long-run nationwide program. Even a very large saturation study might only pick up a small portion of this effect.

The capture claim and **the reduced-capture-corruption-and-bureaucracy claim(s)** cannot be tested in an experiment because they involve market reactions and/or the internal workings of a potential future government administration. The bureaucratic structure needed to run a small-scale, temporary experiment will provide no evidence about the bureaucratic structure needed for a large-scale, permanent national program or about the behavior of public employees within that structure. To the extent that these claims involve capture by private economic entities such as employers and landlords, an RCT will provide no direct evidence and a saturation study will provide very little. Labor markets are primarily national. The effect of geographically dispersed, randomly selected individuals will be nonexistent. The effect of geographically concentrated subjects in a saturation study will probably be much smaller than the national response, and how large it is will depend on how isolated the community is.

The labor-productivity claim, **the increased-innovation-and-entrepreneurship claim**, and **the better-working-conditions claim** are extremely hard to observe because they depend on the long-term reactions of both recipients and employers. Researchers can examine whether people in a short-term experiment seek training or education, whether they are healthier, and so on, but they will be unable to observe whether and how any gains in these areas will eventually affect workers' productivity, entrepreneurship, and mobility. A major part of the argument for increased labor productivity and improved working conditions is through employers: a decline in labor effort gives employers incentive to increase wages, improve working conditions, and introduce higher productivity techniques. Because RCTs are unable to observe employer responses, they cannot observe whether this path actually leads to higher productivity or better working conditions. The best they can do to approach employer reaction is to observe whether the UBI trial leads to a decline in labor-market participation, which is only the first step in the chain expected to lead to these results.

Similarly, researchers can observe part of the first step of **the structural-disadvantage claim** and **the dynamic-efficiency claim** (does it improve education, childhood health and nutrition, entrepreneurship, and so on). A major part of the first step is true by definition: that UBI can reduce poverty. A great deal of theory and empirical evidence indicate that people who grow up and live with a reduced threat of poverty are much better able to succeed in ways that benefit themselves and others. The majority of claims on the UBI supporters' list are closely tied by theory and past observations to the structural-disadvantage claim. Unfortunately, experiments cannot directly observe whether these first steps toward reducing structural disadvantages do in fact lead to the dynamic process needed to produce greater efficiency or reduced disadvantage.

Yet these issues, especially the structural-disadvantage claim, cannot be left out of the discussion. The elimination of structural disadvantage is an important concern for any country that endorses the principle of equality before the law. It would be an enormous example of the streetlight effect if people involved in the discussion got distracted by quantitative comparison of how much the control and experimental groups work or drink from the important question of whether experimental evidence is connected by theory to good reasons to believe that UBI will have a significant effect on the structural causes of poverty, inequality, and other forms of disadvantage.

The flexible-lifestyle claim, **the productive nonlabor claim**, **the gender-role-reinforcement claim**, **the degrowth claim**, **the consumerism claim**, and **the self-destruction claim**, all share two problems. They require observing behavior that is not easy to observe and making subjective and/or normative judgments about that behavior. For example, researchers can observe whether parents use their UBI to spend more time with children and whether women do this more often than men, but they will not be able to observe whether this reaction should be seen as reflecting increased flexibility in lifestyles or as reinforcement of gender roles. It will be very difficult to observe whether test subjects react in ways that lead to more or less growth and consumerism. Even if researchers are able to observe what subjects do with increased available nonlabor time, researchers would have to make controversial moral judgements to label that time "productive," "unproductive," or "self-destructive."

Yet, researchers will need to find some nonjudgmental way to make findings about subjects' behavior relevant for these debates. For example, although they should avoid making moral judgments, they should not avoid estimating whether UBI is correlated with alcohol or drug abuse.

In addition, most of these variables depend heavily on long-term and community effects. For example, the ability of a person using a UBI to adopt a more flexible lifestyle is likely to depend on factors such as whether the UBI is permanent and whether it affects the market and culture in ways that make flexible lifestyles more feasible and attractive. Any short-run observations of people in a small-scale experiment are likely to give little indication of the long-run reaction to a national UBI for any of these possible effects.

The economic-stimulus claim, the economic-impediment claim, and associated subclaims involve market reaction to UBI, which RCTs cannot observe at all and saturation studies can observe only partly. Some of the potential effects involved are macroeconomic, operating at the national and—in the Eurozone—at the supranational level. A small-scale experiment can say nothing about them. Evidence has to be gathered from other sources.

The shut-door claim, the increased-support-for-redistribution claim, and **the decreased-overall-redistribution claim** involve the way voters and policymakers feel about and respond to UBI at the national level over time. Experiments provide no evidence about them.

The migration claim fits largely into this category as well. If immigrants are eligible for a substantial UBI shortly after they arrive, it's reasonable to think more immigrants will want to come. But most countries control their immigration and the eligibility rules for immigrants. So, they can choose whether and when immigrants become eligible and whether or not to allow increased immigration. Regional polities that do not control their migration from other parts of the country and are required by national rules to extend eligibility to migrants might face this issue, as might countries, such as European Union members, that have signed international agreements allowing free migration across national borders and prescribing when and whether immigrants from treaty countries are eligible for redistributive programs. But whether a UBI increases immigration to these countries is not something a UBI experiment (which has to have fixed control and experimental groups) can test.

Although **the politically-enabled-proletarian claim** and **the bought-off-proletarian claim** are potentially observable in an experiment by comparing the political behavior of people in the experimental and control groups, there are at least four reasons to believe it is beyond the reasonable capability of an experiment. First, political behavior is extremely difficult to observe and hard to quantify. Second, community effects are likely to be substantial. The way one person behaves politically affects their fellow citizens' behavior. Third, once a national UBI is in place, it would change the political dialogue and political behavior in unpredictable ways. Fourth, the long-term political response after years of activity and discussion in a national policy setting is likely to be very different from the initial reaction of study subjects.

Nevertheless, researchers should be aware that these claims affect how people interpret the other experimental results. Suppose the experimental group works fewer hours than the control group. This result could be a good thing because it is the first step in a process consistent with the anti-exploitation claim, the better-working-conditions claim, the reduced-capture claim, the labor-productivity claim, the productive nonlabor claim, the degrowth claim, the capture claim, the consumerism claim, and the politically-enabled-proletarian claim. But this result could be a bad thing because it is the first step in a process consistent with the exploitation claim, the gender-role-reinforcement claim, and the economic-impediment claim. People who feel strongly about these issues are likely to see confirmation in the results, glossing over the distance between the first step that might be confirmed by the experiment and the final step required for their theory to produce the result they expect. Keeping people from making this leap is a difficult challenge for anyone writing about experimental findings.

The difficulty of relating the trial findings to the issues being debated might tempt researchers to report experimental results on their own terms without any comment on what they indicate for all these different debates, but as past experience shows, ignoring these debates makes it easier for people to spin the results one way or another.

CHAPTER 16

Claims That Can Be Tested but Only Partially, Indirectly, or Inconclusively

Abstract This chapter discusses claims that can be examined by Universal Basic Income (UBI) experiments but shows that each of them can only be tested partially, indirectly, and/or inconclusively. It discusses the implications these limitations have for conducting a UBI experiment and communicating its results.

Keywords Basic income experiments • Negative Income Tax experiments • Social science experiments • Basic income • Universal Basic Income • Inequality • Poverty

This chapter addresses claims that can be tested, but shows that they can only be tested partially, indirectly, or inconclusively. No claims from the list in Chap. 13 can be tested fully, directly, and reasonably conclusively in a small-scale experimental setting the way medicines can sometimes be tested. The central question is how to deal with the indirect and partial nature of the findings.

Experiments have some ability to examine the following claims:

- The welfare claim
- The economic-equality claim
- The reduced-social-costs claim

K. Widerquist, *A Critical Analysis of Basic Income Experiments for Researchers, Policymakers, and Citizens*, Exploring the Basic Income Guarantee, https://doi.org/10.1007/978-3-030-03849-6_16

- The labor-effort claim
- The affordability claim
- The poverty-trap claim
- The harm-to-workers claim
- The benefit-to-workers claim
- The widespread-benefit claim
- The cost-effectiveness claim

1 The Welfare Claim

The welfare claim is probably the most important empirical claim in the UBI debate. The central reason to support a transfer payment is to make people better off. Although some past studies have underplayed the welfare question in favor of more easily measurable variables, the ability of UBI to achieve that goal is far more important than its potential side effects.

Welfare—an abstract concept about people's inner state—is not directly observable. The best existing methods for determining welfare are self-assessments and observations of quality-of-life indicators. Welfare is at least partly subjective, and some quality-of-indicators can be morally loaded. Alcohol is clearly unhealthy and has many potentially damaging side effects, but if it has no ability to increase welfare, 70% of Americans don't know what's good for them.

Fortunately, many quality-of-life indicators are not as tricky. If you have more secure access to an adequate diet, more secure housing, fewer feelings of social isolation, and healthier, longer-lived children than otherwise, you are almost undoubtedly happier. People who are happier with an inadequate diet, ill-health, shorter-lived children, and so on probably suffer from a diagnosable mental disorder. And so, we can safely use many quality-of-life indicators.

Social scientists have developed reasonable welfare indexes based on well-researched indicators.[1] Researchers conducting UBI experiments can report on quality-of-life indicators in a nonjudgmental way and employ respected indexes to provide an overall measure of welfare. They can also conduct a survey asking people in the control and experimental groups about their well-being and about factors likely to affect it.

One important aspect of welfare that could be particularly important to UBI experiments is time use. UBI has the potential to free up people's time.

[1] For a discussion of indicators of basic needs, see Karl Widerquist, "The Physical Basis of Voluntary Trade," *Human Rights Review* Online First (2008).

If so, will people spend more time in education, childcare, volunteering, positive social relationships, or various behaviors that might be labeled as "lazy" or "self-destructive?"

The need for welfare indicators means that the welfare claim is a host of claims and subclaims. I haven't attempted to list each claim separately because there are too many of them, including effects on physical and mental health, homelessness, housing quality, infant mortality, education, food security and adequacy, nutrition, problems associated with the "ghettoization" of poverty, and many more.

Researchers could straightforwardly employ standard quality-of-life indicators and welfare indexes, but they might also consider addressing welfare issues that have particular importance to the UBI debate, such as those related to the freedom claim, the flexible-lifestyle claim, the consumerism claim, and the self-destruction claim. I've discussed the difficulty of dealing with these claims, but they do affect welfare and have particular importance to the UBI discussion in many countries.

The sheer volume of welfare indicators that one can put into an index distracts attention from how important each of them is. I'm guilty of that, leaving most of them out of the list of named claims. But UBI experiments must emphasize all quality-of-life indicators they can measure and explain the relationship between them and the ones they can't.

The difficulty of observing, measuring, quantifying, and combining quality-of-life indicators into a good understanding of welfare discourages work on it. But it has to be the central focus of any attempt to find out whether UBI succeeds in achieving its central goal. By contrast, the labor-time comparison between the control and experimental groups, though far less important, attracts attention because it is a nice, neat, apparently-easy-to-understand number.

Community and long-term effects on welfare are likely to be substantial because there are so many channels by which UBI is likely to affect welfare: direct distribution, market effects on income and working conditions, reduced inequality, reduced ghettoization of poverty, improved education, and so on. Researchers will have to do a great deal of extrapolation to relate study findings to reasonably accurate predictions for a national program. Individual-level RCTs will underestimate the impact of UBI on quality-of-life indicators—both positive and negative. Saturation studies will do only slightly better. Most welfare effects are likely to accumulate slowly over the long term, to be larger for a policy expected to be permanent, and to involve national-level community effects.

One advantage of saturation studies is that some welfare-related community effects are local. A 5–10-year saturation study in an impoverished town—if feasible—could produce a great deal of information about the effects of ghettoized poverty, not just about UBI's role in alleviating it.

The trial will give some indication about the direction of UBI's impact on various welfare indicators, but researchers will have to extrapolate using other evidence to estimate the welfare impact of a national UBI, including the feedback effects from employers and the community over the long run. Those predictions will be based largely on that other evidence, but experiments can provide useful information about the direction of change.

2 The Economic-Equality Claim

The economic-equality claim, as stated, needs no test because UBI necessarily reduces inequality through direct redistribution as long as it is set at a sustainable level. But the important issue is not whether but *how much* UBI reduces inequality. This question is partially testable because it depends on many market factors, some of which are observable. But experiments will only reveal the first step in a long chain of reactions that will determine UBI's effect on economic equality. Experiments can compare the incomes of people in the control and experimental groups, but they will need to combine that with evidence from other sources for UBI's likely effects on taxes paid by higher-income people and on employers' wage response. Some kind of simulation will be necessary, and this estimate will be only the short-term effect of a temporary policy.

To get some idea of longer-term effects, researchers can observe the initial effects of UBI on education, health, safety, food security, and other factors that are correlated with economic mobility, but they cannot actually observe whether those factors do lead to greater economic equality for experimental participants. Researchers can use other evidence about how these variables are correlated to economic mobility to estimate their effect on economic equality, but experimental findings will make only a small contribution to that estimate and the effort becomes somewhat speculative.

3 The Poverty-Trap Claim

The poverty-trap claim implies that UBI will lead to greater labor effort for people eligible for full-time benefits under a conditional system. This can happen because many conditional programs (such as disability, public housing, unemployment insurance, and in the United States, free or subsidized medical care) require people to sacrifice all or most of their benefits if they accept employment or have private income above a certain level. This rule gives recipients a financial incentive to choose benefits over low-paid labor, discouraging them from taking steps toward economic mobility—hence the "trap." Some conditional programs have effective marginal tax rates in excess of 100%, so that recipients are financially better off remaining on benefits than they would be taking a low-wage job.

UBI eliminates the poverty trap because people receive the grant regardless of income. Virtually all UBI proposals are structured so that people are always financially better off earning more than earning less, removing the trap.

A UBI experiment can test reasonably well whether people—in the short term—respond to the removal of the poverty trap at a given wage. But the long-run impact of permanently freeing people from the poverty trap is likely to be much larger. Experiments cannot determine whether improvements in health, education, housing, food security, market conditions, and similar variables increase people's ability to get out of poverty in the long run. Additional theory and evidence will have to be combined with experimental findings to produce an estimate.

For this issue, it is extremely important to separate the effects of the size of transfer from the effects of the type of transfer. If a large UBI is tested against a small conditional program, some or all of the work-stimulating impact of removing the poverty trap will be counteracted by the creation of a more generous alternative to work.

4 The Reduced-Social-Costs Claim

Experiments can address **the reduced-social-costs claim** by examining the demand for social services among experimental subjects. Examples include UBI's potential to alleviate the poverty trap or to improve health and reduce the demand for healthcare. Not all social costs are easily observable, and so the results will be only partial. Experiments cannot reveal the full impact of UBI on the demand for social services because that demand greatly depends on community and long-run effects. Researchers will have to rely on a large amount of nonexperimental evidence to estimate the effect of UBI on social costs.

This issue has been underemphasized in some past experiments because of its difficulty, but it is so important that it must not be ignored. For example, Michael McLaughlin and Mark Rank estimate that the annual cost of US child poverty alone is $1.0298 trillion or 5.4% of GDP,[2] not including the costs of *adult* poverty.

5 The Labor-Effort Claim

Experiments can provide some direct evidence about **the labor-effort claim**, but that evidence can be deceptive. Experiments will observe the difference between the average number of hours worked by the control and experimental groups, and that comparison is likely to attract a lot of attention not only because of the political importance of the labor-effort effect, but also simply because it is easily quantified. "What is the labor-effort response in the experiment?" "It is X%." A simple number that took years of research to produce can be very satisfying, especially to an audience that doesn't understand how far removed the raw comparison of control and experimental groups is from a prediction of the national labor-effort response to a fully implemented UBI system.

Even as a measure of the initial response of workers, this comparison is likely to overstate the effect of a national UBI because, as earlier chapters explained, the sample will probably be drawn from a small segment of the income distribution, including people who are more likely to reduce their labor hours in response to UBI than other segments. Experiments drawing samples in this way will have to bring in nonexperimental evidence to connect their findings to the effect of a national UBI.

It is not certain that UBI experiments will find a correlation between UBI and decreased labor effort. As mentioned above, in less wealthy nations, UBI has been associated with an increase in labor hours, and it might be associated with an increase in labor effort if the sample focuses on people caught in a poverty trap. However, unless a nation has a very large number of people caught in a poverty trap or in extreme poverty, such as that experienced in poorer nations, a slight decline in labor effort is probable and its importance should not be overblown.

The observable reaction of laborers is not the full effect on labor effort even in the short run. As earlier chapters explained, supply and demand theory predicts that the market will react to a decline in labor hours by increasing wages and/or improving working conditions in the relevant sectors, and that each of these effects will cause labor hours to rebound,

[2] Michael McLaughlin and Mark R Rank, "Estimating the Economic Cost of Childhood Poverty in the United States," *Social Work Research* 42, no. 2 (2018).

partially counteracting the initial decline. RCTs cannot directly observe the labor-demand response at all, although they can use a microsimulation model to estimate it. As always, that means that the experimental findings play a lesser role in determining the final estimate—much of which will come from the assumptions going into the model. Saturation studies can capture some demand response, but only at the local level, which is likely to be much smaller than the national demand response.

Even these simulations will produce incomplete results because the input data involves only the short-term response of workers to a temporary program. The long-term response of workers and employers cannot as easily be estimated with simulation techniques because it depends on unpredictable cumulative changes in variables, such as improved health, education, housing, cultural norms, bargaining power, food security, and so on.

Yet the simulations need to be run, and any possible unmeasurable long-term effects explained and perhaps predicted on an ad hoc basis, because of the central role labor effort has for many critics of UBI and because of its vulnerability to spin and misunderstanding. Recall from Chap. 6 that the labor-effort effect dominated the public discussion of the NIT experiments of the 1970s. The raw comparison of the control and experimental groups was discussed in the popular press as if it were a straightforward representation of the national response, when in fact the national response was estimated to be two-thirds smaller. This issue dominated the discussion and distracted attention from more important issues.[3] Anyone reporting or writing about future experiments should try to preempt a repeat of this misuse of experimental findings.

Writers can help by pointing out that the labor-effort claim is not merely the claim that UBI reduces labor hours; it is the claim that the fall in labor effort is "unacceptably high." The definition of unacceptable is subjective and morally loaded. UBI supporters are likely to define "acceptability" synonymously with sustainability, connecting it with affordability (see discussion below). At least some opponents are likely to define it so strictly that they can present *any* decline in labor effort as unacceptable. In the absence of a shared understanding of the controversy over the acceptability criteria, many writers during the 1970s discussion tacitly assumed that any decline in labor hours was unacceptable—regardless of how large or small that decline was and seemingly all other factors.[4]

[3] Moffitt; Widerquist, "A Failure to Communicate: What (If Anything) Can We Learn from the Negative Income Tax Experiments?"

[4] "A Failure to Communicate: What (If Anything) Can We Learn from the Negative Income Tax Experiments?" Also see Chap. 6.

UBI experiments in wealthy nations will probably find a decline that is "acceptable" by the sustainability standard and "unacceptable" by the no-decline-is-acceptable standard, giving each side the opportunity to spin the results their way. Researchers can help head off this kind of spin by recognizing that the controversy over acceptability criteria exists and by addressing it directly. They can discuss the relevance of the experimental results to people with each of these points of view and look for other standards that might be of interest to people with more moderate views.

Alternative standards of acceptability might involve other questions, such as: how much of the decline was composed by workers reducing their hours, by unemployed workers increasing their search time, or by people leaving the labor force? How do they spend their increased nonlabor time, as full-time caregivers, as students, as entrepreneurs, and so on? What costs and benefits are associated with this decline in average labor effort? Is the decline in labor effort something that can be counteracted by other factors, such as an increase in the number of available jobs that offer high wages and good working conditions?

6 The (Un)Affordability Claim and the Cost Issue in General

Experimental evidence can play a small but worthwhile role in addressing **the (un)affordability claim** and other issues relating to cost. For any given UBI scheme, cost can be assessed in terms of taxes and in terms of efficiency loss. Cost can be viewed in terms of taxes or in terms of efficiency, which is discussed above.

The direct tax cost of UBI can be calculated fairly well with income statistics. That is, determine how much UBI costs assuming no one changes their behavior in response to it or to the tax increases that will accompany it. I've elsewhere estimated that a UBI of $12,000 has a net cost less than 3% of GDP, and a UBI of $20,000 has a net cost less than 10% of GDP.[5] The role of experiments is to help determine how changes in behavior affect that cost. A negative labor-effort effect increases cost. An increase in wages or a decline in the need for other social services (via desirable effects on health, education, crime, etc.) will decrease costs. The effects of social costs are too large to ignore, no matter how difficult they are to estimate. I've quoted figures showing that the annual cost of US

[5] "The Cost of Basic Income: Back-of-the-Envelope Calculations."

child poverty is 5.4% of GDP.[6] That savings alone would more than pay for the $12,000 UBI and would relieve more than half of the cost of the $20,000 UBI.

Experiments estimate only the first step in the chains of reactions that lead to these results. Simulation models can help estimate some of the further steps.

The contribution of experimental data to the cost issue is so small that one could imagine using nonexperimental data to estimate labor-market responses in a microsimulation involving no experimental data at all, but microsimulations are also a highly imperfect method. Experimental findings need to be understood as an effort to improve estimates of some of the parameters that go into the model necessary to estimate cost.

The indirect effects on the cost of UBI through its effects on crime, education, health, nutrition, housing, and similar variables are so hard to estimate accurately that the best theoretical models will invariably leave some out and apply speculative estimates of others. But yet they're extremely important. They are likely to have a major impact on the cost of a national UBI. These effects can't be left out of the discussion without badly misinforming nonspecialists, most of whom will not grasp their importance without help.

The question "is UBI affordable?" is too vague to be meaningful. It requires two moral judgments to become meaningful. First, it requires an affordability criterion: how much is too much? Unfortunately, the affordability criterion is subjective and partly morally loaded. UBI supporters (and perhaps others who are positively inclined toward UBI) are likely to define the affordability synonymously with sustainability. That is, a program is unaffordable only if costs associated with it are so large that they collapse the program itself. Opponents (and others negatively inclined toward it) are likely to define the affordability criterion in such a way that *any* added cost is "unaffordable." Many other criteria are possible, and many open-minded people might not have settled on an affordability criterion.

Second, the question is not simply whether UBI is affordable; it is whether the *desired* level of UBI is affordable. Some low level of UBI is clearly affordable (e.g. $1 per year), and some high level is clearly unaffordable (e.g. anything exceeding per capita income). We need to answer the question: how much is enough? Virtually all UBI supporters prefer a UBI high enough to live on—at least to live free from homelessness and economic destitution.

[6] McLaughlin and Rank.

That level is very likely to be sustainable in the context of universal education, healthcare, and other government services provided free-at-the-point-of-delivery as well as policies to ensure that affordable food, housing, and other basics are available in the market.

Eliminating destitution would be an important achievement, but it is not necessarily enough for all or most UBI supporters, most of whom want a UBI that frees everyone from the threat of poverty, ensures everyone a life in dignity, and protects them from significant social exclusion by lack of economic means. Whether that level of UBI is affordable depends both on the affordability criterion and on how generously these conditions are defined.

Researchers conducting experiments cannot hope to resolve these disputes, and they probably should not impose their own criteria on top of the controversy. But they can examine questions that are relevant to the different ways that people who are interested in the UBI discussion view cost and affordability. These might include: how much does a UBI at the official poverty level cost? Is it sustainable or affordable? How much does a significantly higher UBI cost? Is it sustainable or affordable? What is the highest sustainable UBI level? How much will UBI's labor-market and welfare effects increase or decrease its overall cost? What is the efficiency cost of UBI? How do the tax and efficiency costs of UBI compare to the cost of other programs capable of achieving similar goals? What affordability criteria are relevant in the local discussion of UBI? What levels of UBI are part of the local discussion of UBI? How much do they cost and are they sustainable?

Existing evidence overwhelmingly indicates that a UBI high enough to eliminate absolute poverty is sustainable in high-income countries. It won't hurt to double-check the sustainability, but the sustainability of absolute-poverty-level UBI is not a pressing source of serious disagreement in the debate. A sensational media headline saying "Study finds poverty elimination possible with UBI" would be true, but it would not report a groundbreaking finding. Such a headline would spin the discussion of research findings to the pro-UBI side. Yet, leaving UBI's ability to eliminate poverty out of the discussion of the findings spins the issue to the anti-UBI side.

The poverty claim is useful in framing research questions around the cost-effectiveness claim. The question "what is the cost of eliminating poverty with a UBI" is fairly neutral. But a noncomparative focus on cost creates a spin opportunity for the anti-UBI side.

However good the numbers might be, they are not likely to resolve the controversy because are likely to fall into a range where supporters (using a sustainability criterion) can declare UBI "affordable" and opponents (using a criterion putting UBI last on the list of priorities) can declare it "unaffordable." Researchers and anyone else writing about the experiments can help head off spin by recognizing the controversy over the affordability criteria. For example, they can report that the cost of this UBI scheme is affordable by these controversial criteria and unaffordable by these other equally controversial criteria. They can also consider how UBI compares in affordability to other programs of similar size and/or effectiveness—that is, by connecting the affordability question to the cost-effectiveness question.

7 The Widespread-Benefit Claim

The widespread-benefit claim, as I use it, is distinct from the harm-to-workers and benefit-to-workers claims (discussed next). It is not simply the claim that UBI's direct and indirect benefits are shared by many people (whether workers or not) at any given time, but also that a significantly greater portion of people will benefit from UBI at some time in their lives.

The spread of UBI's direct financial benefits at any one time is determined largely by its structure. UBI proposals with feasible costs can be structured so that 40–60% of the population receive direct financial benefits.[7] This much is sufficient to say that a large portion of the population benefits at any one time. There are at least three ways in which UBI's benefits might be spread more widely.

First, because of economic mobility, many more people can expect to benefit financially from UBI at some time in their lives than at any one time—that is, many more people's incomes will go below the break-even point at some point in time. Simply counting contributors and beneficiaries can give the impression that these categories are fixed. Presumably the UBI system is a net benefit to people at the times when they need it most—that is, when they have the least. The question of how many people can expect to benefit at some time during the course of their lives is clearly as important as the question of how many people benefit at any given time.

Second, UBI might create more favorable market or social conditions that directly benefit net financial contributors. (See the benefit-to-works

[7] Widerquist, "The Cost of Basic Income: Back-of-the-Envelope Calculations."

claim below.) For example, the psychological impact of permanently removing the fear of poverty and destitution could benefit everyone.[8]

Third, positive community effects of UBI might benefit net contributors enough to counteract the loss of the taxes they pay. Although it's overly ambitious to hope everyone will benefit all-things-considered, there is evidence that more equal societies are in many ways better for everyone. Lower crime, more stable communities, less group antagonism, healthier environments, and so on can lead to better outcomes for people across the income spectrum.[9]

Unfortunately, RCTs are unable to provide any direct evidence about the community or psychological impact on net (financial) contributors. A saturation study will do only slightly better. Direct observation of the widespread-benefit claim would require an extremely long-term study involving subjects at all levels of income. Researchers can use historical evidence about economic mobility to estimate how many people will fall into the net recipient range at some point in their lives. Experiments can make two small contributions toward understanding this claim by observing the labor-effort effect and UBI's impact on welfare factors likely to improve economic mobility, safety, health, education, and so on. Of course, these are only the first steps in a chain that might benefit net contributors over time.

Again, UBI experiments can only contribute a small piece of evidence to the effort to make these estimates, but a focus on how people benefit throughout their lives is essential to a good public understanding of UBI's likely effects.

8 The Harm-to-Workers Claim and the Benefit-to-Workers Claim

The harm-to-workers and **benefit-to-workers claims**—as stated—are oversimplified. Any UBI system financially benefits some workers and harm others. The relevant questions seem to be: which workers benefit and how much? Which workers are harmed and how much? Is there evidence that a group of people will abandon all "work" (however defined); if so, how many will, and how will this group affect workers?

[8] Erich Fromm, "The Psychological Aspects of the Guaranteed Income," in *The Guaranteed Income: Next Step in Socioeconomic Evolution?*, ed. Robert Theobald (New York: Doubleday, 1966).

[9] Wilkinson and Pickett.

Of course, not everyone agrees that the existence of such a group is ethically problematic, and research should avoid giving off the impression that it necessarily is.

These claims also present at least two difficult subjective definitional issues. First, what do we mean by harm and benefit? Financial harm and benefit are easier to observe and quantify than overall benefit, but they aren't as important. And so, it is best to consider both.

Second, what is a "worker?" Is a full-time parent or caregiver a worker? Are other unpaid workers "workers?" Is a person living off financial investments a worker? How many hours per week does a part-time laborer have to be employed to count as a worker? How many weeks can someone be unable to find a job and still count as a worker? Is a person who uses UBI for a 1-year sabbatical from a 40-year working life a worker? Do children, the retired, and the disabled count as "workers?" And so on. If we define any of these groups as workers, the number of workers UBI benefits will be much higher than if we don't. And even if we don't, we might judge the financial harm these groups create for workers differently than the harm other nonworkers create for workers. This ambiguity is why most of this book avoids the term "worker" altogether in favor of the clearer term "laborer" (meaning a person working for pay). But this section uses "worker" because the ambiguous idea is what matters for the discussion of these claims.

Experiments can say *something* about these claims, but researchers need to approach them cautiously because what they can say is very limited, easily misinterpreted, and connected to contentious ethical disagreements, such as the exploitation debate. Researchers can't ignore them because experimental findings might be misunderstood or spun as showing much more about these claims than they actually do.

As with the affordability claim, experimental evidence plays only a small role in calculating the harm and benefit to workers. Most of the financial harm and benefit of a UBI system is determined by its structure and does not need a test. If UBI is largely income tax financed, anyone making less than the break-even point financially benefits and anyone making more is financially harmed. Other ways of financing UBI make the break-even point more difficult to calculate, but all financing methods create winners and losers.

The last section mentioned that a UBI system can be structured to directly benefit 40–60% of the population (including a lot of workers) at any given time. The direct financial harm to workers in the low end of the net contributory range will be small and might be overridden by positive community effects. Many workers will be in the net beneficiary range at some point in their lives. Also, not all net contributors will be workers. Some will be people living off investment income.

Researchers can help avoid misunderstanding by presenting findings for various demographic groups and various definitions of workers. What percentage of workers are financially harmed? What percentage are financially helped? What is the average net benefit to the average net beneficiary worker? What is the average net harm to the average net contributory worker? What are the average before-and-after-tax-and-transfer incomes to the average net beneficiary worker and the average net contributory worker? What percentage of UBI net benefits go to people in other demographic categories of interest to the discussion, who might not be expected to be laborers? These might include children, caregivers, retirees, students, and so on.

Researchers will understandably reject making the controversial judgment of identifying a group of people as those who could work, should work, and don't work under UBI. But they can better help improve the public understanding by trying to find some nonjudgmental way to report numbers that usefully inform people who have different ethical positions on these issues. One way might be to report the percentage of the cost caused by the benefits to people in the various demographic categories relevant to the national discussion.

Most of the experimental contribution to the understanding of financial harm to net contributory workers is determined by its contribution to our understanding of the total cost of UBI. Policymakers can choose to spread that burden in many different ways, some of which would put most of the burden on rent-paying assets rather than on labor income. This difference will have different implications for people with different moral positions.

Workers working less is the first step *both* in the story ending in worker harm *and* in the story ending in worker benefit. The ability to work fewer hours or take more time to search for the right job if one happens to become unemployed is a direct benefit to workers, but this also increases the tax cost of UBI, some of which might be borne by workers. Theory predicts that employers respond to initial reductions in labor effort by improving pay and working conditions, possible even for net contributory workers. Even if increased wages only go to net recipient workers, it (and any positive response in labor time) will mitigate some of the tax cost of the initial decline in labor time. Estimating the extent to which these factors are both benefits and costs to workers can help avoid misunderstanding.

Trials will contribute to the understanding of the costs and benefits to workers through possible reductions in social costs and through possibly improved worker productivity (see above).

If labor-market response of workers is small, the financial harm and benefit to workers will be pretty much dictated by the structure of the program. If not, other evidence will be required to estimate whether those changes increase or decrease the benefit to net contributory workers. Researchers would need to run a simulation model using nonexperimental estimates of the elasticity of supply and demand in various labor markets. And of course, the outcome of any such model will be somewhat speculative, driven largely by the assumptions of the model. But experimental data is still useful, potentially indicating which segments of the labor market (in terms of occupation, income level, etc.) will be most affected.

9 The Cost-Effectiveness Claim

Although **the cost-effectiveness claim** is the bottom line, it requires little additional discussion because it is examined by putting together the evidence discussed above. Each variable discussed above can be looked at individually in cost-effectiveness terms, and all the variables of interest can be indexed into one overall cost-effectiveness estimate. Combining experimental, historical, and theoretical information to address the cost-effectiveness question makes the results one step less direct and conclusive, but it is more important to report less conclusive answers to meaningful questions than more conclusive answers to less meaningful or misleading questions.

CHAPTER 17

From the Dream Test to Good Tests Within Feasible Budgets

Abstract This chapter discusses possible ways to test Universal Basic Income in light of the issues discussed in previous chapters. It works down from the dream test that solves all testing problems to tests that might be possible within the experiment's budget.

Keywords Basic income experiments • Negative Income Tax experiments • Social science experiments • Basic income • Universal Basic Income • Inequality • Poverty

The past three chapters make a lot of suggestions about what tests should look for. This chapter discuses testing techniques, starting with the dream test and working down toward more feasible tests, making broad recommendations about how to design and report on UBI and related experiments.

The "dream test" is not something a sane person would dream about but an experiment, for which money, time, and political will are not obstacles, allowing social science researchers to test the effect of UBI on a *nation* the way medical researchers test the effects of medicine on individuals. Imagine all humanity shares a desire to test UBI at the national level, and they care more about testing it than about whether they actually live under a UBI system. They are able to maintain this shared political will for generations. Under *those* circumstances, they can do a very good test

K. Widerquist, *A Critical Analysis of Basic Income Experiments for Researchers, Policymakers, and Citizens*, Exploring the Basic Income Guarantee, https://doi.org/10.1007/978-3-030-03849-6_17

indeed. They can divide the 200 or so nations of the world into several control and experimental groups, receiving UBI, the existing systems, equally sized expanded versions of existing systems, and perhaps another policy that UBI is to be tested against. This experiment combines RCT and saturation study techniques with enough saturation sites to ensure statistical significance for virtually any variable of interest. Researchers could then run the test for 50 or 100 years—as long as it takes for long-term effects to play out.

This logically-possible-but-utterly-infeasible experiment solves virtually all of the empirical problems discussed throughout this book. All those national-level community effects and all those long-term effects that obscured the relevance of experimental data for every claim considered above would no longer be obstacles. Such an experiment differentiates between the effects of the size and type of policy being studied. Most of the variables identified above would become testable in a statistically useful way. A few empirical problems remain, such as observational difficulties, the inherent inexactness of statistics, and the problem that it is much easier to produce definitive answers for quantitative questions than for qualitative questions.

But the observable, empirical differences between the experimental and control groups would become so apparent that it is hard to believe anyone would lack the evidence they need to make up their mind. Pretty much the only remaining disagreements would be entirely ethical in character, and we might learn so much that ethical positions might begin to converge.

This experiment might be able to make do with less than all the world's countries and less than a half a century, but we don't work down from this test to a feasible-sized experiment without losing the ability to observe many or perhaps most of the long-term, national-level community effects that the UBI discussion hinges on. Yet, if we simply drop those difficult-to-test variables from consideration, we do the scientific equivalent of looking under the streetlight.

Therefore, perhaps, the second-best test of a UBI is to introduce it in a single country. This test would sacrifice the ability to *control* for anything, but it maintains the ability to observe all the relevant effects of UBI and is an excellent form of trial and error. Is it better to make controlled observations of a few of UBI's effects or uncontrolled observations of all its effects? The answer depends on the importance of the effects lost in the controlled experiment and on what other techniques are available to account for the lack of control in national implementation.

Iceland is a country of only 335,000 people. It would make an excellent national saturation site. GiveDirectly's study in Kenya includes 16,000 people, making it larger than some of the world's smallest countries. The Seychelles has a population of only 94,000 people, some of whom are in such deep poverty that one could imagine wealthy nations (or even a wealthy institution, just six times the size of GiveDirectly) paying the Seychelles to introduce a national UBI on an experimental basis.

The most-promising possibility along these lines is not a national-level *experiment* but the hope that some country decides on its own to introduce UBI as a full-fledged policy, providing a natural experiment. There is little downside to one country introducing UBI at a low level, ratcheting it up slowly, and cautiously observing its effects. But waiting for this to happen has obvious drawbacks as a research strategy.

The next best (and probably still too expensive) study is a full combination of RCT and saturation techniques. The experimental and control groups would each need to be comprised of 30–40 communities to control for unobserved differences between sites, and it would be best to have 30–40 additional communities receiving a more generous version of existing programs—or whatever program UBI is being tested against—to help tease out difference between size and type of program being studied.

In most ways, saturation sites would be selected to be demographically representative of the nation as a whole in as many ways as possible. But, isolated communities might be preferred to more representative sites because, as Chap. 4 mentioned, they will reveal community effects more similar to those we can expect at the national level. Researchers might want to focus on poorer communities because those are the ones where UBI will have the most important impact, but this choice makes the results very different from national results, creating the need to extrapolate from other sources to get national estimates.

As large as the integrated RCT and saturation study would be, it nevertheless loses the ability to estimate the many national-level community effects of UBI. Although isolated sites have community effects somewhat more like those at the national level, they are almost certainly much smaller. However, community effects that occur at the local level are important, especially in impoverished areas, and so a test like this is worth doing if feasible.

Although studies integrating RCT and saturation techniques are likely to be prohibitively expensive in wealthier nations, they are possible in relatively poor countries. The Indian experiment used multiple saturation sites. GiveDirectly's study in Kenya is the first with enough saturation sites to statistically control for unobserved differences between communities. Researchers are making at least some effort to differential between the effects of size and type of policy.

If 30–40 saturation sites are unaffordable (which they usually will be), the next best experiment might be a combination of one saturation study and one individualized RCT. It would be better to have a third site to test UBI against an equal-sized expansion of the existing system, alternative policies, and/or alternative levels of UBI, but the expense may prohibit these and limit the study to one experimental site and one control site.

The word "control" is a bit of a misnomer for a saturation study that has too few sites to control for differences between the sites. For example, imagine that after the study began, the largest employer in the control site went out of business, causing a surge in unemployment. A simple comparison of employment hours in the two communities would say a lot more about the effects of the loss of that employer than about UBI. If something this dramatic happens, researchers will take account of it in ways that are highly imprecise; but the bigger issue to statisticians is unobserved differences between sites. The primarily value of an RCT is its unique ability to control for unobserved factors.

Yet, a saturation study is valuable at this level. It provides uncontrolled observations of local community effects, while an RCT alone provides no observation at all of local community effects. Uncontrolled observations are better than no observation. By running one study of each type researchers can get controlled observations of individual effects and uncontrolled observations of local community effects.

One way to increase the reliability of a saturation study is to begin observing the two communities a year or two before flipping a coin to see which one becomes the experimental site and which one becomes the control. This method effectively allows the site receiving UBI to be tested both against the control site and against itself before the introduction of UBI. There might always be unobserved factors that cause divergence between the two communities to begin at the same time as the UBI, but this strategy reduces the likelihood.

The difficulties of saturation studies notwithstanding, a second "town without poverty" could make a valuable contribution to the contemporary UBI discussion. A saturation study is no more expensive than an RCT of similar size, and it would be an opportunity for at least one of the experimental efforts to make a very different type of observation. With 5–10 experiments happening in wealthy countries, researchers have the possibility of experimenting with very different techniques. It would be a shame if none of the experiments in higher-income nations included a saturation site.

If a saturation study is not possible, individualized RCTs will have to go it alone. The RCT is a good, scientific technique. Unfortunately, it is one that is not able to give direct answers to many of the questions relevant to the public discussion of UBI. This shortcoming does not make an RCT useless for studying UBI, but it does make it far more difficult to conduct and report the results of a UBI experiment in ways that truly enlighten the public discussion of UBI.

As I've stressed, it would be best to test UBI against an equal-sized increase in the existing system and/or one or more equal-sized alternative policies, but as I've also stressed, funding bodies are likely to balk at this option because it roughly doubles the cost of the experiment. One hope along these lines is that some people have begun calling for a test of the government-guaranteed job. A test with two experimental groups (one eligible for UBI, the other for a guaranteed job) as well as a control group (eligible for the current system without expansion) would not answer all the questions about the observed effects that are caused by the size and type of these two policies, but it would reveal a lot about both.

The expense of having two experimental groups will make most funding bodies insist on a simple RCT with one experimental group (perhaps divided between people receiving various levels of UBI) and one control group (eligible for the current system without expansion). This is the model of most past tests in wealthier nations, but it has very little ability to differentiate between the effects of the size and type of policy being studied.

Unfortunately, the size-versus-type issue is one issue on which computer simulations don't make a good substitute for experiments because it affects the initial comparison of the control and experimental groups, which computer simulations usually take as their starting point.

Researchers conducting or writing about UBI experiments can best deal with this shortcoming and all the problems discussed throughout this book by confronting them and never ignoring them. This strategy has implications both for the design and for the reporting of an experiment.

For design, the people commissioning the experiment should consider the test not as a stand-alone project, but as part of a wider effort to learn as much as we can about UBI. Ian Shapiro argues that good social science research should start with a problem, identify what is known about it from the existing stock of theory and empirical knowledge, and then try to design a research strategy to improve that knowledge.[1] This strategy is very different from the process in which, as Chap. 9 argues, we seem to have started with a technique and then asked what that technique does best. It's not too late to partially reverse that process if we focus on how an experiment can contribute to a better public understanding of the most important empirical issues in the UBI discussion.

That is, start with the bottom-line question and all the specific issues that are relevant to the bottom line and/or important to the local discussion of UBI. What do we want to know about UBI? What do we know from existing theory and evidence? How can experimental evidence, in combination with existing theory and evidence, extend that knowledge? How does that effort run short? What controversies remain?

Chapters 12, 13, 14, 15, and 16 have made an effort to identify many testable claims and research questions that can help in this effort, but no one should take my word for it. The discussion varies extensively from place to place and time to time. As argued above, it is important both to heed the lesson here and to formulate questions relevant to the current local discussion.

One interesting way to settle on a list of research questions would be to hold a meeting of people on all sides of the discussion to find out what empirical questions they want answered. It will be difficult for any such group to be (recognized as) truly representative, but if people with very different positions on UBI can at least agree to map out the empirical disagreements that divide them, they can give researchers a good idea of what empirical questions are important to the discussion. It is extremely important to ask them what they most want to know *about UBI* rather than what they would most like to learn *from an experiment*. Framing the question toward a list of things experiments are good at doing is the equivalent of directing everyone's attention to the area under the streetlight. Tailor the research to the empirical questions at issue; do not tailor the questions to the answers research techniques are good at finding.

Once a list of things we want to know is identified, it becomes possible to ask what experiments can contribute to improving our understanding of them. This puts the experiment in the context of how it needs to be supplemented by observational evidence, theory, and qualitative discussion and interpretation.

[1] Ian Shapiro, "Methods Are Like People: If You Focus on What They Can't Do, You Will Always Be Disappointed," in *Field Experiments and Their Critics: Essays on the Uses and Abuses of Experimentation in the Social Sciences*, ed. Dawn Langan Teele (New Haven, CT: Yale University Press, 2014), p. 238.

For reporting the results, this book has stressed throughout that researchers need to go beyond a simple report on the differences between the control and experimental groups because of its vulnerability to misunderstanding, spin, and sensationalism. They also need to abandon the belief that any list of caveats can bridge the gap between such a report and a genuine understanding of the experiment's implications for the important issues. Caveats cannot do that job. A second round of analysis is needed.

This second round of analysis, like most social science research, involves using theory that infers causal links from correlations found in past observational evidence.[2] I only know of four alternative methods: (1) the back-of-the-envelope method, making calculations assuming no one changes their behavior; (2) computer simulation techniques using theory based on evidence from past experiments and observations; (3) laboratory experiments (as opposed to field experiments)[3]; and (4) qualitative, ad hoc, logical, heuristic discussion of the probable causes and effects involved. The effort to combine experimental findings with findings from these methods involves econometrics, general equilibrium computer simulation modeling, and qualitative analysis, all of which are far outside my area of expertise, and so I can give only a very bare overview.

Researchers need to estimate the response of all potential laborers, not just those in the demographic groups from which the study subjects were drawn and not just those in the market at any given time, but all people who might work more or less in response to the UBI or the taxes used to finance it. Researchers have to estimate the tax cost of the (different levels of) UBI in question and consider at least one or perhaps several different taxation methods, and then estimate how these parameters affect the marginal incentives of workers and investors. They need to obtain estimates of the elasticities of demand and supply of labor and use them in general equilibrium analysis to estimate the new equilibrium wage and quantity of hours worked and how that might shift in the long run. Observational data will probably contribute more to that overall discussion than experimental data because most existing data on most topics is observational.[4]

Microsimulations do not eliminate the need for caveats, they merely change the nature of the caveats involved. Instead of explaining why experimental findings don't answer the questions people most want answered, the

[2] Van Parijs and Vanderborght, pp. 144–145, have a similar discussion.

[3] Although lab experiments are popular in economics, they might not useful for the study of UBI.

[4] Gelman, pp. 192–3.

caveats would have to explain three other things: (1) the limited role the experimental findings played in the answers given to those questions; (2) the sources, quality, and role of the other evidence used; and (3) the techniques employed to combine the evidence. These caveats also risk being misunderstood. The devil is in the caveats.

To say that experimental evidence plays a small part in that kind of analysis does not mean its contribution is trivial. The tools exist, but like experimentation, microsimulation is a highly imperfect technique. The outcome of a computer simulation is as good as the assumption that goes into it, and social science has extremely limited ability to firmly estimate any parameter that might be used in a simulation.

A similar process can be used to estimate the impact of UBI on quality-of-life indicators. Researchers then can go on to a qualitative discussion of the importance of the estimates obtained through such simulations. Interactions between variables are important for that kind of discussion. For example, if people do in fact work less, what do they do with their time and what is the moral relevance of that shift in time-use for people with different ethical positions? What is the meaning behind the change in the quality-of-life index.

Researchers also need a qualitative discussion of the reliability of the estimates presented. For example, how does the inability to separate the effects of the size and type of policy being studied affect our judgment of UBI from this study? How much evidence is there that the parameters entered into the models are accurate? Even if accurate, how might they change as culture reacts to the introduction to UBI?

More importantly, research reports need a qualitative discussion of things that can't be estimated with these techniques. For example, if experiments find that UBI is good for nutrition, education, mental and physical health, housing equality, crime reduction, domestic violence reduction, and so on, how are these changes likely to affect structural disadvantage, persistent inequality, and other important goals of distributive policy. No econometric model can estimate all of these changes, as a society takes years to react to a new economic policy, but these issues are centrally important to the UBI discussion. This discussion should bring in lessons learned from nonexperimental programs, such as the Alaska Dividend, conditional cash transfers, Native American casino dividends, and many other relevant experiences.

A report with analysis of this kind is only the first step in overcoming all the issues involved with successfully enlightening the public understanding. The other steps involve what happens when the issue gets into the public sphere. I'll address that in the final chapter, but first I'll address the question of whether we should bother to have an experiment at all when experiments have so many limitations.

CHAPTER 18

Why Have an Experiment at All?

Abstract This chapter considers whether it is, after all, worthwhile (both strategically and scientifically) to have a Universal Basic Income (UBI) experiment, given that earlier chapters have shown so many difficulties experiments have in addressing the most important issues in the public discussion of UBI.

Keywords Basic income experiments • Negative Income Tax experiments • Social science experiments • Basic income • Universal Basic Income • Inequality • Poverty

This book's goal is to examine the many potential pitfalls of UBI experiments, so that people learn more from the experiments we're doing. The book is not about whether experiments are after all a good idea. I'm largely neutral on this question, but given the many shortcomings I've pointed out, I feel obliged to consider it. You can approach it both scientifically and strategically.

Strictly speaking, science cannot tell you whether to do anything or not. That depends on your values. But I can think of at least three ways to approach this question from a scientific perspective.

K. Widerquist, *A Critical Analysis of Basic Income Experiments for Researchers, Policymakers, and Citizens*, Exploring the Basic Income Guarantee, https://doi.org/10.1007/978-3-030-03849-6_18

First, can science settle the disagreement? It can't, but cases where experiments can settle disagreements are rare. The distance from experiments and other research methods to anything like a bottom line is a common methodological problem across the social sciences.[1] To expect it on an issue like this is to expect more than most social science can deliver.

Second, do UBI experiments add to our understanding of this policy? Certainly, what they can do is limited and tentative, and to get people to truly understand the contribution they do make, researchers will have to point out how limited and tentative their contribution is, but doing so risks giving people the impression that they aren't very valuable at all.

Perhaps the most compelling reason to use the experimental method for an issue like this is, because "all the available methods of studying politics are pretty bad."[2] Given the limitations of the four other methods mentioned in Chap. 17, it's plausible that field experiments can make a valuable contribution. Enlightening the discussion with improved evidence requires open-minded self-reflection on the limits of what each method contributes to our understanding, which will still be limited even as evidence gradually improves it.[3]

Experiments aren't great, but neither are micro- or macro-economic simulation models. There are lot a of unknowns about this largely untried policy (UBI). An experiment—used in combination with other also-limited methods—is a way for social scientists to fill in a few of those gaps, while a lot of unknowns remain. If we think UBI experiments—or any other social science method—can do more than that, we have unrealistic expectations.

There is no strong, scientific downside to conducting an experiment. It's not prohibitively expensive or dangerous to the subjects. Most of the past experimental evidence available on UBI is very specific to the time and place where it was gathered. If one polity conducts a UBI experiment, it can learn something about how UBI works relative to existing alternatives in that context. If many different polities experiment with UBI, we can hopefully piece that information together into a slightly better shared understanding of UBI's effects in more general terms.

[1] Deaton and Cartwright.

[2] Shapiro, p. 228.

[3] Dawn Langan Teele, "Introduction," ibid., p. 4; Susan Stokes, "A Defense of Observational Research," ibid.

Third, one can ask whether there is a scientific *need* to conduct an experiment. Would it be irresponsible for policymakers to seriously consider this policy without testing it first, the way we learned that it was irresponsible to allow the sale of Thalidomide to pregnant women without adequate testing? Here the answer is clearly no. While there is no strong, scientific downside to conducting an experiment, there is no strong, compelling downside to introducing UBI without further experimentation. Most major policy changes are simply rolled out without advanced experimentation. And this roll-out can begin modestly and increased gradually, while policymakers fix problems as they come up.

UBI is certainly compatible with this kind of process. *Some* level of it is sustainable; *some* level isn't. For UBI to be unsustainable would require not just some reduction in work effort, but a massive labor-market withdrawal that made essential industries unprofitable in ways that could not be counteracted either by automation or by enticing workers back to the labor force with better wages and working conditions. This process does not seem likely even with a substantial UBI. And if it seemed to be moving that way, we could simply reduce the UBI to a more modest level. I suspect the bigger problem with UBI would be the political difficulty of raising it to a level that is high enough rather than cutting it back if it is unaffordably high.

The strategic question is very different: will good scientific research help demonstrate the efficacy of UBI and attract support? Perhaps, but experiments have a lot of risks for UBI supporters. Even if experiments are good science and find promising results, Van Parijs and Vanderborght warn of the possibility of "damaging backlash analogous to the one that followed the North American experiments."[4] Others worry about a double standard: why is UBI subject to so much testing when most social policy is rolled out with little or no advanced experimentation?

Although UBI supporters may be rational to desire the immediate introduction of UBI, that is still an uphill battle. At the rate the UBI movement has grown over the last few years, that could change, but at the moment, UBI remains an outside long shot, and experiments are a strategic attempt to build the movement further. I've argued that the Namibian and Indian experiments played an important role in sparking the current UBI movement.[5] Whether the 5–10 experiments getting underway will

[4] Van Parijs and Vanderborght, p. 143.

[5] Widerquist, "Three Waves of Basic Income Support."

push the movement further remains to be seen. They provide the opportunity for UBI supporters to show they're interested in evidence-based reasoning and are willing to subject their idea to testing and revision if necessary.

Evaluating experiments as a political action requires comparing them to other strategies to promote UBI. In this sense, UBI experiments come off very well because, for the most part, they are not coming at the expense of the other things supporters are doing to promote it. If you're a major donor to Y Combinator, the Economic Security Project, or GiveDirectly, this strategic question might be important for you. If you're anyone else, you can look at the experiments as a bonus. UBI supporters are free to go on with just as much activism as before. As long as the experiments have even a minor contribution to the UBI movement, supporters can consider them a publicity windfall.

Although the risk that experiments will backfire exists, not all experiments have backfired, and past experience provides lessons on how to resist backlash this time. I don't think either researchers or UBI supporters are capable of controlling the reaction to experimental findings to prevent negative spin. And they are not immune to doing their own spin. But I do think they're better prepared to handle it fairly than researchers or BIG supporters were in the 1970s.

And we should not look at the 1970s experiments as negative on the whole. The media response at the time was negative, but the NIT movement was already in serious decline before the major negative media discussion got under way. The mere fact that government conducted these experiments has given BIG credibility ever since. And the popular understanding of the 1970s experiments has greatly improved in the last 10–15 years. Even if the experiments had a net negative effect on the BIG discussion at the time, perhaps, by now, they have had a net positive impact on the current UBI movement.

Finally, the question of whether we should have UBI experiments is moot. We are having them now. We are having them not because of a careful consideration of strategic or scientific perspectives on why to have an experiment, but because of the complex political process discussed in Chap. 9. The question is not whether to conduct an experiment, but how to make the best of the experiments being conducted now.

CHAPTER 19

Overcoming Spin, Sensationalism, Misunderstanding, and the Streetlight Effect

Abstract This chapter concludes with a discussion of how to work forward from the results of Universal Basic Income (UBI) experiments to the public discussion in ways that overcome communication barriers and reduce the problems associated with them. It argues that it is not enough to communicate the findings of experiments on their own terms, but results have to be presented with an understanding of the role they play in the political economy of the UBI discussion. Researchers must relate experimental findings to the most important questions in the evaluation of UBI, even if experimental findings make only a small contribution to the search for those answers.

Keywords Basic income experiments • Negative Income Tax experiments • Social science experiments • Basic income • Universal Basic Income • Inequality • Poverty

Reporting the findings of a UBI experiment is extremely difficult because oversimplification is inherently easier to understand than genuine complexity. No person or group created this problem. It results from the complexity of the issue and the diversity of the people involved in the discussion. The effort to overcome spin, sensationalism, misunderstanding, and the streetlight effect will never be perfect. But there are things everyone

K. Widerquist, *A Critical Analysis of Basic Income Experiments for Researchers, Policymakers, and Citizens*, Exploring the Basic Income Guarantee, https://doi.org/10.1007/978-3-030-03849-6_19

involved can do to reduce these problems. This concluding chapter brings together and completes lessons on this issue from throughout this book.

Everyone involved can help by recognizing how difficult it is to understand each other when the discussion involves people as diverse as citizens, activists, elected officials, appointed public servants, managers, researchers across diverse fields, science communication specialists, professional journalists, amateur journalists, and so on. Many people fit more than one category, but those who do cannot instantly solve the communication issue. The first step, as I've argued, is to work backward from the public discussion of UBI to the experimental design.

Citizens involved in the discussion can help this effort by going beyond the blanket demand for an experiment and trying to get a realistic picture of what they hope to learn. Citizens' ability to do this is limited because the public discussion involves millions of people who have very different political views and are not organized into a body. But writers within the movement can write about what specifically they want to learn from a UBI trial. Organizers can organize online or in-person public discussions of what people want to learn from UBI trials.

The people who commission the experiment and the public servants, managers, and researchers who design and conduct it can help by consciously trying to understand and respect the public discussion of UBI. The main goal of a broad-based study should be to enlighten the public discussion with evidence people can understand. Even if the study is intended to be a narrowly focused, technocratic approach to a few specific questions, it will be a part of the public discussion, and making the results understood should be one of its goals.

This suggestion does not mean that experiments must attempt to answer every UBI-related question people might have, no matter how unanswerable. It means that the public discussion can be taken into account in the design of the study and the reporting of its findings. Chapters 12 and 13 discussed claims that are important to the discussion around the world. Chapters 14, 15, and 16 suggested how to orient experiments toward these claims, even though experiments cannot definitively answer them. Foremost among these is the very reasonable desire to relate all of the experiments' findings to the bottom line: what do they contribute to the overall evaluation of UBI as a policy option?

My list of claims is no substitute for a good understanding of the discussion in the relevant political context. Not all the claims listed in Chap. 13 are relevant everywhere and additional claims will be relevant in most places. People designing tests should learn as much as they can about the local discussion, but knowledge of it is not always a good reason to ignore this book's advice. Researchers can err on the side of caution by being more reluctant to subtract than to add to that list.

Three issues in specialist-nonspecialist communication are likely to have implications for experimental design in most political contexts.

First, the public discussion often conflates ethical and empirical issues. Empirical researchers naturally focus on empirical questions, but they too often sweep ethical questions under the rug. Researchers can best separate these issues by bringing them into the open. People with different ethical perspectives are interested in different empirical claims and often use very different criteria to evaluate empirical findings. Framing the issue in one way or another can advantage one side or another's spin on the results. A study could strive for a truly neutral framing, but it might be better off providing information that is useful to people with different ethical perspectives relevant in the political context and discussing the finding in relationship to those opposing perspectives.

Second, people involved in the public discussion are exclusively interested in the long-term impact of a permanent, national UBI on almost any variable an experiment might study. They have no direct interest in the simple comparison between the control and experimental groups in temporary experiments. No list of caveats, no matter how well written, can convert knowledge of that simple comparison into a genuine understanding of its implications for a permanent, national UBI. Without a second round of analysis and clear discussion of what it does and does not imply, research will misinform nonspecialists.

Bridging this gap requires bringing in evidence from other sources to make predictions about how community effects are likely to play out in the short and the long run. It requires more qualitative discussion of the study's findings. It requires researchers to be unafraid of calling attention to the uncertainty of the study's predictions and to the smallness of the contribution experiments make to our overall understanding of UBI. But it is necessary to help the public discussion benefit from the contribution that experiments make.

Third, as this book stresses throughout, research reports have to discuss the questions they can't answer, including the big, bottom-line questions: does it work; should we do it? Although it is naïve to hope experiments can fully answer those questions, ultimately, those are the right questions—the things we need to know when we consider introducing a policy. Even the most technically focused research question is important to the extent that it contributes to that overall evaluation.

In the absence of an answer to the bottom-line question, researchers can relate their findings to it: examine whatever aspects of it experiments can, both alone and in combination with other evidence, techniques, and theories. Then discuss the potential impacts of the things their research cannot examine. The political nature of UBI experiments and the inherent difficulty of the material make this effort essential, even if less-politically oriented research is free from this concern.

The effort to work backward is especially important to avoid the streetlight effect. People designing UBI experiments might want to ask themselves: are we focusing on these questions because they are the most important aspects of the overall evaluation of UBI or because they are the easiest questions to answer with the techniques we have? Attention to the overall public evaluation of UBI might refocus the study toward variables that experiments can address only partially and toward more qualitative methods.

Researchers should not neglect answering the questions trials are best able to answer, and they might have an extremely good reason for narrowly focusing their study on issues that differ considerably from those of most interest to the public discussion, but to avoid misunderstanding, they need to clearly explain two things: why they are studying what they are studying rather than the issues of most interest to the public discussion and the extent to which their findings help answer those questions. Research reports need to appreciate how difficult these issues are for nonspecialists and that they have historically been the source of misunderstanding.

The bottom line is important also because it forces comparison of costs and benefits. Discussion of benefits in isolation biases the reaction one way; discussion of costs in isolation biases it the other way—even if the existence of that effect was highly predictable and the experimental question about it was merely how large it would be. To head off this problem when reporting on—say—a decline in labor effort, researchers need to address what that decline means in human terms, whether it can be counteracted by other factors (such as a healthy macroeconomy), what people are doing with their time, and what the likely market response to that decline means for wages, working conditions, education, and so on. These issues need to be addressed not simply to avoid misunderstanding, but also to make research useful.

Once the study is completed, the effort to work forward again to the public discussion begins. People writing about the results might have a more difficult job than is typical in science communication. It is not enough simply to help people understand the experiments on their own terms—for example, what an experiment is, what control and experimental groups are, and what differences were found between the control and experimental groups. They have to explain the relevance of those findings to the most important issues in the public discussion in ways people can understand.

Many common errors in understanding are predictable. For example, whether because of sensationalism or professional deference, some people are likely to interpret experimental results as more conclusive than they are. Whether because of a desire to spin or overconfidence in the meaning of research, some people are likely to discuss various results out of context as if they were votes in favor or against the adoption of UBI nationally.[1]

People directly involved in the experiments are not the only ones who can help create a better public understanding of the findings. Anyone with good knowledge can help improve public understanding, making themselves heard—and understood—to counteract any spin and misreporting. Outside researchers who understand the place of experiments in the political economy of the UBI discussion can reexamine and represent findings in ways they recognize as more useful and less likely to be vulnerable to spin or sensationalism.

Journalists, bloggers, and anyone interested in writing about UBI trials usually have no special training in understanding the policy implications of technical experimental findings. But they can help by taking time to investigate the difficult issues involved and by trying to avoid the easy and sensational oversimplification.

Citizens—it could perhaps go without saying—can help by exploring the diverse literature that will be produced on UBI experiments and reading it critically.

[1] See Chap. 6 for how this happened for the labor-market findings of the 1970s experiments.

Bibliography

Ashenfelter, O. 1978. The Labor Supply Response of Wage Earners. In *Welfare in Rural Areas*, ed. J.L. Palmer and J.A. Pechman. Washington, DC: Brookings Institution.

Atkinson, Anthony. 1995. *Public Economics in Action: The Basic Income/Flat Tax Proposal.* Oxford: Clarendon Press.

Bishop, J.H. 1979. The General Equilibrium Impact of Alternative Antipoverty Strategies. *Industrial and Labor Relations Review* 32 (2): 205–223.

Bouquin, S. 2005. Social Minima in Europe: The Risks of Cumulating Income-Sources. In *The Ethics and Economics of the Basic Income Guarantee*, ed. Karl Widerquist, M.A. Lewis, and S. Pressman, 212–231. Aldershot: Ashgate.

British-Columbia-Government. 2018. Researchers Explore the Potential of Basic Income in B.C. Victoria. *BC Gov News.*

Burtless, G. 1986. The Work Response to a Guaranteed Income. A Survey of Experimental Evidence. In *Lessons from the Income Maintenance Experiments*, ed. A.H. Munnell. Boston: Federal Reserve Bank of Boston.

Cain, G.C., W. Nicholson, C. Mallar, and J. Wooldridge. 1974. The Labor-Supply Response of Married Women, Husbands Present. *Journal of Human Resources* 9 (2): 201–223.

Colini, Laura. 2017. The B-Mincome Project Journal No 1, 23. Barcelona: The City of Barcelona.

Condliffe, Jamie. 2016. In 2017, We Will Find Out If a Basic Income Makes Sense. *MIT Technology Review*, December 19.

K. Widerquist, *A Critical Analysis of Basic Income Experiments for Researchers, Policymakers, and Citizens*, Exploring the Basic Income Guarantee, https://doi.org/10.1007/978-3-030-03849-6

Deaton, Angus. 2014. Instruments, Randomization, and Learning About Development. In *Field Experiments and Their Critics: Essays on the Uses and Abuses of Experimentation in the Social Sciences*, ed. Dawn Langan Teele, 141–184. New Haven: Yale University Press.

Deaton, Angus, and Nancy Cartwright. 2016. Understanding and Misunderstanding Randomized Controlled Trials. In *NBER Working Paper Series*, ed. National Bureau of Economic Research. Cambridge, MA: National Bureau of Economic Research.

Forget, Evelyn L. 2011. The Town with No Poverty: The Health Effects of a Canadian Guaranteed Annual Income Field Experiment. *Canadian Public Policy* 37 (3): 283–305.

Forget, E.L., Dylan Marando, Michael Crawford Urban, and Tonya Surman. 2016. Pilot Lessons: How to Design a Basic Income Pilot Project for Ontario. In *Mowat Research*. Toronto: Mowat Centre.

Fromm, Erich. 1966. The Psychological Aspects of the Guaranteed Income. In *The Guaranteed Income: Next Step in Socioeconomic Evolution?* ed. Robert Theobald, 183–193. New York: Doubleday.

Gelman, Andrew. 2014. Experimental Reasoning in Social Science. In *Field Experiments and Their Critics: Essays on the Uses and Abuses of Experimentation in the Social Sciences*, ed. Dawn Langan Teele, 185–195. New Haven: Yale University Press.

Greenberg, D.H. 1983. Some Labor Market Effects of Labor Supply Responses to Transfer Programs. *Social-Economic Planning Sciences* 17 (4): 141–151.

Groot, Loek F.M., and Timo Verlaat. 2016. The Rationale Behind the Utrecht Experiment. Utrecht University School of Economics.

Haarmann, Claudia, Dirk Haarmann, Herbert Jauch, Hilma Shindondola-Mote, Nicoli Nattrass, Ingrid van Niekerk, and Michael Samson. 2009. *Making the Difference: The Big in Namibia: Basic Income Grant Pilot Project Assessment Report*. Windhoek: Basic Income Grant Coalition.

Hanlon, Joseph, Armando Barrientos, and David Hulme. 2010. *Just Give Money to the Poor: The Development Revolution from the Global South*. Boulder: Kumarian Press.

Houser, Kristin, and June Javelosa. 2017. Bill Gates: The World Isn't Ready for Universal Basic Income Now, but We Will Be Soon. Futurism.com, February 28.

Hum, D., and W. Simpson. 1993. Economic Response to a Guaranteed Annual Income: Experience from Canada and the United States. *Journal of Labor Economics* 11 (1, part 2): S263–S296.

Johnson, Paul. 1998. Parallel Histories of Retirement in Modern Britain. In *Old Age from Antiquity to Post-modernity*, ed. Paul Johnson and Pat Thane, 211–225. London: Routledge.

Kangas, Olli. 2016. *From Idea to Experiment: Report on Universal Basic Income Experiment in Finland*. In Working Papers, 62. Helsinki: Kela.

———. 2017. *Final Report for the Finnish Basic Income Experiment Recommends That the Experiment Be Expanded*. Helsinki: Kela.

Kangas, Olli, Miska Simanainen, and Pertti Honkanen. 2017. Basic Income in the Finnish Context. *Intereconomics* 52 (2): 87–91.

Keeley, M.C. 1981. *Labor Supply and Public Policy: A Critical Review*. New York: Academic.

Kluve, Jochen. 2010. The Effectiveness of European Active Labour Market Programs. *Labour Economics* 17 (6): 904–918.

Levine, Robert, Harold Watts, Robinson Hollister, Walter Williams, Alice O'Connor, and Karl Widerquist. 2005. A Retrospective on the Negative Income Tax Experiments: Looking Back at the Most Innovative Field Studies in Social Policy. In *The Ethics and Economics of the Basic Income Guarantee*, ed. Karl Widerquist, Michael A. Lewis, and Steven Pressman, 95–106. Aldershot: Ashgate.

McCambridge, Jim, John Witton, and Diana R. Elbourne. 2014. Systematic Review of the Hawthorne Effect: New Concepts Are Needed to Study Research Participation Effects. *Journal of Clinical Epidemiology* 67 (3): 267–277.

McFarland, Kate. 2017. Overview of Current Basic Income Related Experiments. *Basic Income News*, October 19.

McLaughlin, Michael, and Mark R. Rank. 2018. Estimating the Economic Cost of Childhood Poverty in the United States. *Social Work Research* 42 (2): 73–83.

Miller, Annie. 2017. *A Basic Income Handbook*. Edinburgh: Luath Press Limited.

Ministry-of-Community-and-Social-Services. 2018. In *Ontario's Basic Income Pilot: Studying the Impact of a Basic Income*, ed. Ontario Ministry of Community and Social Services. Toronto: Queen's Printer for Ontario.

MIT-Technology-Review. 2018. *What We Do*. Cambridge, MA: MIT Technology Review. https://www.technologyreview.com/about/. Accessed 1 June 2018.

Moffitt, R.A. 1979. The Labor Supply Response in the Gary Experiment. *Journal of Human Resources* 14 (4): 477–487.

Rees, A., and H.W. Watts. 1976. An Overview of the Labor Supply Results. In *Work Incentives and Income Guarantees: The New Jersey Negative Income Tax Experiment*, ed. J.A. Pechman and P.M. Timpane. Washington, DC: Brookings Institution.

Reynolds, Matt. 2018. No, Finland Isn't Scrapping Its Universal Basic Income Experiment. *Wired*, April 26.

Robins, P.K. 1980a. Labor Supply Response of Family Heads and Implications for a National Program. In *A Guaranteed Annual Income: Evidence from a Social Experiment*, ed. P.K. Robins, R.G. Spiegelman, S. Weiner, and J.G. Bell. New York: Academic Press.

———.1980b. Job Satisfaction. In *A Guaranteed Annual Income: Evidence from a Social Experiment*, ed. P.K. Robins, R.G. Spiegelman, S. Weiner, and J.G. Bell. New York: Academic Press.

———. 1984. The Labor Supply Response of Twenty-Year Families in the Denver Income Maintenance Experiment. *Review of Economics and Statistics* 66 (3): 491–495.

———. 1985. A Comparison of the Labor Supply Findings from the Four Negative Income Tax Experiments. *Journal of Human Resources* 20 (4): 567–582.

Robins, P.K., and R. West. 1980. Labor-Supply Response Over Time. *The Journal of Human Resources* 15 (4): 524–544.

SEED. *A Guaranteed Income Demonstration*. Stockton: Stockton Economic Empowerment Demonstration. https://www.stocktondemonstration.org/

Shapiro, Ian. 2014. Methods Are Like People: If You Focus on What They Can't Do, You Will Always Be Disappointed. In *Field Experiments and Their Critics: Essays on the Uses and Abuses of Experimentation in the Social Sciences*, ed. Dawn Langan Teele, 228–241. New Haven: Yale University Press.

Standing, Guy. 2008. How Cash Transfers Promote the Case for Basic Income. *Basic Income Studies* 3 (1): 1–30.

———. 2012. Basic Income Pilot Schemes: Seventeen Design and Evaluation Imperatives. In *Wege Zum Grundeinkommen* [*Pathways to Basic Income*], ed. D. Jacobi and W. Strengmann-Kuhn, 133–152. Berlin: Bildungswerk Berlin.

———. 2013. *Unconditional Basic Income: Two Pilots in Madhya Pradesh*. In Conference on Unconditional Cash Transfers: Findings of Two Pilot Studies, 1–7. New Delhi: Sewa.

———. 2017. *Basic Income: And How We Can Make It Happen*. New York: Penguin.

Stokes, Susan. 2014. A Defense of Observational Research. In *Field Experiments and Their Critics: Essays on the Uses and Abuses of Experimentation in the Social Sciences*, ed. Dawn Langan Teele, 33–57. New Haven: Yale University Press.

Teele, Dawn Langan, ed. 2014a. *Field Experiments and Their Critics: Essays on the Uses and Abuses of Experimentation in the Social Sciences*. New Haven: Yale University Press.

———. 2014b. Introduction. In *Field Experiments and Their Critics: Essays on the Uses and Abuses of Experimentation in the Social Sciences*, ed. Dawn Langan Teele, 1–8. New Haven: Yale University Press.

Torry, Malcolm. 2016. *The Feasibility of Citizen's Income*. New York: Palgrave Macmillan.

Van Parijs, Philippe, and Yannick Vanderborght. 2017. *Basic Income: A Radical Proposal for a Free Society and a Sane Economy*. Cambridge, MA: Harvard University Press.

Watts, H.W., R. Avery, D. Elesh, D. Horner, M.J. Lefcowitz, J. Mamer, D.J. Poirier, S. Spillerman, and S. Wright. 1974. The Labor-Supply Response of Husbands. *Journal of Human Resources* 9 (2): 181–200.

Widerquist, Karl. 2005. A Failure to Communicate: What (If Anything) Can We Learn from the Negative Income Tax Experiments? *The Journal of Socio-Economics* 34 (1): 49–81.

———. 2006. The Bottom Line in a Basic Income Experiment. *Basic Income Studies* 1 (2): 1–5.

———. 2008. The Physical Basis of Voluntary Trade. *Human Rights Review*, August 30. Online First.

———. 2017. The Cost of Basic Income: Back-of-the-Envelope Calculations. *Basic Income Studies* 12 (2): 1–13.

———. Forthcoming. Three Waves of Basic Income Support. In *Palgrave International Handbook of Basic Income*, ed. Malcolm Torry. New York: Palgrave Macmillan.

Widerquist, Karl, and Michael W. Howard, eds. 2012a. *Alaska's Permanent Fund Dividend: Examining Its Suitability as a Model.* New York: Palgrave Macmillan.

———, eds. 2012b. *Exporting the Alaska Model: Adapting the Permanent Fund Dividend for Reform Around the World.* New York: Palgrave Macmillan.

Widerquist, Karl, Jose Noguera, Yannick Vanderborght, and Jurgen De Wispelaere. 2013. *Basic Income: An Anthology of Contemporary Research.* Oxford: Wiley-Blackwell.

Wilkinson, Richard G., and Kate Pickett. 2009. *The Spirit Level: Why More Equal Societies Almost Always Do Better.* London: Allen Lane.

Y-Combinator-Research. 2017. *Basic Income Project Proposal*, 32. Oakland: Y Combinator Research.

Index[1]

[1] Note: Page numbers followed by 'n' refer to notes.

K. Widerquist, *A Critical Analysis of Basic Income Experiments for Researchers, Policymakers, and Citizens*, Exploring the Basic Income Guarantee, https://doi.org/10.1007/978-3-030-03849-6

W

Y

The manufacturer's authorised representative in the EU is Springer Nature Customer Service Centre GmbH, Europaplatz 3, 69115 Heidelberg, Germany. If you have any concerns regarding our products, please contact ProductSafety@springernature.com

Printed and bound by CPI Group (UK) Ltd, Croydon, CR0 4YY

30/09/2026

02225260-0016